INTERCESSIONS
FOR A

A hundred jargon-free prayers for
public worship and personal devotion

NICK FAWCETT

kevin
mayhew

kevin
mayhew

First published in Great Britain in 2017 by Kevin Mayhew Ltd
Buxhall, Stowmarket, Suffolk IP14 3BW
Tel: +44 (0) 1449 737978 Fax: +44 (0) 1449 737834
E-mail: info@kevinmayhew.com

www.kevinmayhew.com

9 8 7 6 5 4 3 2 1 0

ISBN 978 1 84867 915 3
Catalogue No. 1501553

Cover design by Rob Mortonson
© Image used under licence from Shutterstock Inc.
Typesetting by Angela Selfe
Proofread by Sarah Stanley

Printed and bound in Great Britain

Contents

About the author

Brought up in Southend-on-Sea, Essex, Nick Fawcett served as a Baptist minister for thirteen years, and as a chaplain with Toc H for three, before deciding to focus on writing and editing, which he continues with today, despite wrestling with myeloma, an incurable cancer of the blood. He lives in Wellington, Somerset, with his wife, Deborah, and – when they are home from university – his two children, Samuel and Kate. Delighting in the beauty of the West Country, Nick and Deborah love nothing more than walking stretches of the South West coast path at weekends, and Nick – as well as finding time for online games of chess and Scrabble alongside his many editing commitments – finds constant inspiration for his numerous books in the lanes and footpaths near his house. His aim, increasingly, is to write material free of religious jargon that reaches out to people of all faiths and none.

Introduction

Does intercession 'work'? Honestly, I don't know. Can it possibly make any difference? Again, I don't know. I've wrestled with precisely such questions through much of my life, and wrestle with them still. But if I don't have all the answers, I'm convinced nonetheless that interceding for others is vital. It's about caring, expressing our concern for others, and surely that should be a central concern of people of all faiths and none. If responding to the needs of our world doesn't matter to us then what on earth are we about?

Intercession is not about changing God's mind, as though God can somehow be persuaded of the merits of a case if only we berate him long enough or ensure sufficient people are praying for the same thing at the same time. It's not about reminding God about a particular person or situation, as though their needs may somehow have slipped the divine memory. Such a God would be a whimsical monster, undeserving of praise or worship. No, intercession is as much for our benefit as for God's. It reminds us of matters we sometimes ignore or forget. It brings home the reality of human need. And it prompts us into action. Those facets alone offer a more than sufficient validation of intercession.

So how do we go about it? Too often, intercessory prayers are vague and wishy-washy – 'Oh Lord, we pray for the wider world and all its needs' – as though that covers everything. Or, in worship and prayer meetings, we are subjected to rambling and tedious prayers that never seem to end, as though every situation imaginable must be included in case God has somehow overlooked them. For me, such approaches take us back to false ideas of what intercession is all about. God knows the needs of the world whether we articulate them or otherwise, but intercessory prayer helps us to tune into them, to identify ourselves with such needs, and to start answering our prayer by sharing in God's transforming work – caring, sharing, giving, helping; offering ourselves as his hands and feet.

In this book, I provide a hundred all-new prayers on specific themes – situations of human need that, sadly, all too frequently rear their head or that are simply part of daily life for many. My aim is to provide a resource for whoever is entrusted with leading intercessions in public worship, so that they may pray meaningfully, thoughtfully and confidently.

A second aim in these prayers has been to avoid religious language throughout. That may sound strange for a book of prayers, but I believe it's important, for too often in prayer we can slip into jargon, far more frequently than we may realise. We use terms like 'grace', 'blessing', 'repentance', 'sanctification' and a host of others – words that may mean something to regular worshippers but probably mean nothing at all to those approaching God for the first time. We do so innocently enough, but if we're not careful these become empty words – religious padding to disguise a lack of genuine meaning in the prayers we offer.

Prayer shouldn't be like that. While there's certainly a place on occasions for the language of the Book of Common Prayer – I love that as much as any – we need to pray also in the modern-day vernacular and, as far as possible, in words that speak to non-believers as much as believers. We need to *include* rather than *exclude*, to welcome in rather than shut out. That's what I've attempted to do in this book, avoiding jargon as much as possible and using language that, hopefully, can speak to all.

Our hurting world needs praying for as much as ever, perhaps more so. It is our privilege and responsibility to intercede for it and act on our intercessions. My hope is that something in these pages will play a part in making that possible.

Nick Fawcett

PRAYERS

1. Abuse, victims of

(*See also* The exploited and abused)

Lord of all,
we think today of those people,
far too many,
who have been victims of abuse.

We think of those who have been sexually molested
as children,
their innocence taken advantage of,
their place within the home or among wider family and
friends exploited.
We think of the fear, confusion and revulsion such children
must have endured,
and of the mental scars they continue to bear:
the feelings of guilt, disgust and self-loathing,
the memories that refuse to be suppressed,
the hold that the psychological and physical impact of their
experiences continues to have,
so often blighting their lives.
Bring help.
Bring healing.

We think of those who, in a host of ways,
have been abused in later life:
of victims of sexual harassment, stalking or rape,
their confidence undermined,
a cloud of fear and hurt overshadowing all;
of those who live in abusive relationships,
bullied at school, at home, or in the workplace,
each day lived in the fear of fresh indignities;
of those who experience racist or homophobic abuse,
taunted for the colour of their skin,
their creed, their culture, their sexuality –

made to feel that they are outcasts,
rejects,
socially inadequate and inferior.
Bring help.
Bring healing.

We think of those who have abused others,
especially those who have betrayed their responsibilities:
parents and relatives,
bishops, priests and clergy,
media celebrities,
staff of hospitals, orphanages and children's homes.
Give to all in such positions of trust a genuine concern for
all in their charge;
a determination to put their welfare before all else.
Bring help.
Bring healing.

We think of those in hospitals,
care homes and nursing homes,
cruelly or insensitively treated by poorly trained staff,
kept in soiled sheets for hours at a time,
ignored though they are in pain or need of attention,
ridiculed or roughly handled by those lacking in empathy
or patience.
Bring help.
Bring healing.

Give wisdom and guidance to all who seek to prevent abuse;
to weed it out and bring to justice those who have
committed it;
to maintain and improve standards where the vulnerable
are cared for;
and to minister to those who have suffered at first-hand.
Bring help.
Bring healing.
Amen.

2. After a major accident

(Supply relevant details in place of the ellipsis)

God of all,
we bring before you those who have been caught up in the
tragic events of . . . –
all whose lives have been turned upside down
by what has happened,
and who find themselves overwhelmed by fear, confusion,
grief and uncertainty.
Give strength.
Give help.

We think of the families of those who have lost their lives,
reeling from shock and overwhelmed by sorrow;
of those waiting for news of children, partners, parents,
relatives, friends;
of those whose loved ones are in intensive care;
of those whose future has been changed for ever.
Give strength.
Give help.

We think of those scarred in body and mind by what they
have been through,
those still in hospital,
those who have sustained life-changing injuries,
those who are critically ill.
Give strength.
Give help.

We think of those striving to bring order out of the chaos
and hope out of despair:
emergency services,
relief workers,
doctors, surgeons and nurses,
counsellors and carers.
Give strength.
Give help.

We think finally of those who will investigate this accident,
those who will enquire into its causes
and those who will make recommendations as a result of
their findings.
Give patience and wisdom to them all,
so that through the deliberations conducted
and decisions made,
other accidents such as this may be prevented in the future.
Give strength.
Give help.
Amen.

3. Aid agencies

(*See also* Charities)

Lord of all,
hear our prayer for aid agencies
and international relief charities.

We think of aid workers in difficult and dangerous parts of
the world,
sometimes putting their own safety at risk to bring food,
medicine,
supplies,
relief,
to those in need.
Give guidance.
Give help.

We think of those who are dependent on such help,
their survival depending on donations,
food drops,
relief convoys,
provisions reaching them from outside.
Give guidance.
Give help.

We think of relief workers in places afflicted by
natural disaster –
famine,
flood,
earthquake,
tsunami –
and those working in countries torn by war or disease,

striving to help people pick up the pieces of their lives
so that they are able to start again.
Give guidance.
Give help.

We think of those who oversee such work,
taking difficult decisions as to what to do with the
resources available,
who to help and who not to,
how much they can afford to give,
to do
and to continue to budget for.
Give guidance.
Give help.

We pray for those involved in financing aid –
fundraisers,
charity shops,
governments,
corporations,
individual donors –
future work hinging on winning the hearts and
minds of the public.
Give guidance.
Give help.

For all organisations committed to helping the poor,
the needy,
the hurting,
the broken,
we bring our prayer.
Give guidance.
Give help.
Amen.

4. Alcoholics

(See also Drug addicts)

God of love,
hear our prayer for those who have become addicted
to alcohol,
or who may be on the road to dependency.

We think of young people in an increasingly
alcohol-fuelled culture,
not only able to drink in quantities as never before,
but *expected* to do so,
despite the potential impact on their health,
their work,
their relationships,
their future.
Teach them to recognise when enough is enough;
when they need to say no rather than yes.

We think of those in danger of becoming alcoholics in
their own home:
bored housewives;
the bereaved and those seeking solace;
the depressed and lonely;
those seeking to drown out demands of work,
relationships,
self-image
or the daily routine of life.
Teach them to recognise when enough is enough;
when they need to say no rather than yes.

We think of those unable to cope with the pressures of
fame and stardom,
needing ever more Dutch courage,
ever more pick-me-ups
before they feel able to perform,
or sucked into a lifestyle where indulgence in alcohol is the
norm rather than the exception,
until they find they can no longer live without it.
Teach them to recognise when enough is enough;
when they need to say no rather than yes.

We think of those completely in the thrall of alcohol,
unable to get through another day,
even another hour,
without their required fix,
caught in an ever-deepening spiral of decline,
yet unable to drag themselves out of it –
their body broken,
their mind addled,
their life a shadow of what it once was.
Teach them to recognise when enough is enough;
when they need to say no rather than yes.
Amen.

5. Ambulance staff and paramedics

(*See also* Casualty departments; Hospitals)

God of all,
we think today of all who work in the ambulance service.

We pray for paramedics,
so often first on the scene in an emergency,
and we think especially of the challenging situations
they face each day:
critically ill patients in need of immediate treatment;
harrowing sights at the scene of an accident;
abusive and aggressive behaviour putting them at risk.
In all they do,
help them to work wisely and well.

We pray for ambulance drivers,
tasked with reaching patients as quickly as possible,
yet with driving safely at the same time,
and increasingly finding themselves frustrated by a shortage
of resources –
forced to wait outside hospitals while a bed can be found
for their patient,
rather than setting off in response to other emergency calls.
In all they do,
help them to work wisely and well.

We pray for switchboard staff fielding a constant
stream of calls:
each day dealing with anxious family and friends,
with people scared by symptoms they are experiencing,
with some who need talking through
life-saving procedures,
with others who simply need calming down,
and sometimes with hoax callers.
In all they do,
help them to work wisely and well.

We pray for those who train ambulance staff
and paramedics,
who service their vehicles,
who maintain their equipment,
or who must budget for their funding
and allocate the resources needed.
In all they do,
help them to work wisely and well.
Amen.

6. Animal welfare

(*See also* Veterinary surgeons)

God of all,
we pray today for the animals you have given to share this
planet with us,
and for their welfare.

We think of creatures driven to the edge of
extinction by human activity,
hunted for food,
ivory,
so-called medicinal purposes
or purely for sport;
poisoned by gamekeepers, fertilisers or pesticides;
driven from their habitats by logging, burning,
farming or urban development;
threatened by the impact of climate change.
Teach us to celebrate the diversity of life,
and to treat all creatures with respect.

We think of farm animals –
so many cruelly treated across the world,
made to live in inhumane conditions:
caged or battery hens and pigs;
cows bred to produce vast milk yields;
creatures slaughtered inhumanely;
unwanted animals callously disposed of.
Teach us to celebrate the diversity of life,
and to treat all creatures with respect.

We think of household pets,
most of them lovingly cared for,
but some abused by uncaring owners,
thrown out on to the street,
starved,
beaten,
denied exercise and veterinary care,
or kept in horrendous conditions.
Teach us to celebrate the diversity of life,
and to treat all creatures with respect.

We think of those who seek to safeguard
the welfare of animals –
government and international bodies that legislate
concerning standards,
regulations
and punishments for transgressing these;
agencies and charities that campaign against exploitation
and cruelty;
local rangers and volunteers who strive to protect
particular species –
all who work to promote greater respect
for the animal kingdom.
Teach us to celebrate the diversity of life,
and to treat all creatures with respect.
Amen.

7. The anxious

(See also The fearful)

Loving God,
hear our prayer for those plagued by anxiety.

We think of those consumed by financial worries,
wondering how they will get through another week,
how they will put food on the table,
how they will provide for their loved ones,
how they will pay their mortgage or their debts.
Calm their fears,
and grant them true peace of mind.

We think of those worried about loved ones –
about the education,
health,
jobs,
prospects
and well-being of those close to them.
Calm their fears,
and grant them true peace of mind.

We think of those worried about relationships –
about possible infidelity,
about strains and stresses on their marriage,
about sexual performance or hang-ups,
about feuds or divisions,
or about their inability to form the relationships they crave.
Calm their fears,
and grant them true peace of mind.

We think of those who are anxious about the future –
who worry about what it might bring,
the challenges they may have to face
and their ability to cope with them,
the years ahead seen as a threat rather than an opportunity.
Calm their fears,
and grant them true peace of mind.

We pray for those who worry not about anything in particular
but who are simply anxious by disposition,
habitually insecure,
their thoughts constantly troubled,
each day faced with a dark cloud hanging over them,
a shroud of fear and uncertainty.
Calm their fears,
and grant them true peace of mind.

Quieten the hearts of all who are anxious,
and still their spirit.
Teach them to deal with those worries they can address,
and to forget the rest,
letting each day's trouble be sufficient for itself.
Calm their fears,
and grant them true peace of mind.
Amen.

8.   The armed forces

(*See also* War and peace; War, people and places broken by;
World peace)

Loving God,
we bring before you today those who serve in the
armed forces.

We think of those in the Navy,
often spending long months away from home and family,
with all the tensions and pressures that involves;
their work potentially dangerous,
especially in times of war,
with the risk of attack from land, air or sea.
In all they do,
guide and protect them.

We think of those in the Air Force,
their role seen by some as glamorous, exciting,
yet once again involving its own dangers –
of pilot error,
engine malfunction,
an enemy shooting them down
or being trapped in a burning plane.
In all they do,
guide and protect them.

We think of those in the Army,
entrusted with the hands-on business of battle,
the encountering of foe face to face,
the reality of close contact,
the danger posed by snipers, IEDs and suicide bombers,
mortars, shells and rockets,

and the possibility, should they fall into the wrong hands,
of barbaric and brutal treatment.
In all they do,
guide and protect them.

We think of the psychological effects of war on troops –
shell shock,
post-traumatic stress,
Gulf War syndrome,
to name but some –
the awful sense of responsibility at being able to deliver
death in an instant,
of seeing colleagues injured and maimed,
of living with the constant threat of danger.
But we think also of the sense of achievement
in liberating a subject people,
of keeping the peace in places of conflict,
of delivering aid to those in need,
of helping to make possible new beginnings,
free from the yoke of tyranny.
In all they do,
guide and protect them.

Watch over all in the armed forces.
Save them from loneliness and disillusionment,
from poor provisioning and lack of resources,
from jingoism or callousness,
from injury and death.
In all they do,
guide and protect them.
Amen.

9. Arthritis

God of all,
hear our prayer for those who suffer from arthritis.

We think of the many people,
especially those who are older,
afflicted by osteoarthritis –
joints giving them constant pain,
bones aching,
their sleep disturbed,
mobility restricted
and happiness undermined.
Reach out to help.
Reach out to heal.

We think of those taking painkillers for their condition,
those finding temporary relief through steroid treatment,
those taking other forms of medication,
and those waiting for operations –
replacement hips, knees or other joints –
hoping and praying that the surgery
will give them a new lease of life,
freedom from their discomfort.
Reach out to help.
Reach out to heal.

We think of those suffering from rheumatoid arthritis,
many contracting the condition early in life
and seeing it develop with alarming speed,
bringing with it acute pain and often disabling damage –
hard to bear yet harder still to alleviate,
and with no sign yet of a cure on the horizon.
Reach out to help.
Reach out to heal.

We think of GPs and consultants,
seeking to help their patients in whatever way they can;
of surgeons conducting operations
to bring relief and mobility;
of families and friends striving
to offer practical and emotional support;
and, above all, of dedicated charities,
committed to supporting sufferers and helping
to fund research into new treatments,
so that this cruel disease, in its various forms,
may finally be defeated once and for all.
Reach out to help.
Reach out to heal.
Amen.

10. The bereaved

Lord of life,
we remember today those who walk
in the shadow of death,
those wrestling with the trauma of losing a loved one.

We think of those who have lost a partner –
so many memories shared,
so much experienced together,
so much love given and received,
all suddenly cut short,
as though, for the one bereaved, a part of themselves
has gone missing.
Bring comfort.
Bring hope.

We think of children who have lost their parents:
their anchor in life suddenly removed;
a giver of love no longer there to give anything;
a provider able to provide no more;
a guide, guardian and friend lost for ever.
Bring comfort.
Bring hope.

We think of parents who have lost a child –
one they have lovingly nurtured plucked from their grasp,
hopes and dreams snuffed out,
memories now bringing pain as much as pleasure,
an unbearable sense of loss.
Bring comfort.
Bring hope.

We think of all who have lost people close to them –
brothers, sisters, uncles, aunts, grandparents,
friends and colleagues:
all who have been an integral part of life
and whose passing leaves a void impossible fully to fill.
Bring comfort.
Bring hope.

Reach out to the bereaved in their pain and sorrow,
numbness and despair,
shock and disbelief,
and give them the courage, support and strength
they need to cope with the reality of death,
yet to trust that it will not have the final say:
that somehow you are able to bring new beginnings
out of endings –
buried seeds yielding new life,
winter turning to spring.
Bring comfort.
Bring hope.
Amen.

11. Barriers in society, those working to break down

God of all,
hear our prayer for those who strive to break down barriers
in our society –
all who work to overcome the walls of suspicion,
fear and hatred
that divide person from person,
and nation from nation.

We think of those who promote interfaith dialogue –
who seek to end religious intolerance,
bigotry,
fundamentalism
and extremism,
helping believers,
no matter how fervent,
to recognise that there is truth in convictions
other than their own,
that none has a monopoly on the truth.
Whatever divides us,
may much more unite.

We think of those who strive to counter barriers of race –
who work to educate the ignorant,
to challenge discrimination,
to safeguard equality of opportunity,
to bring communities together
and integrate people of all colours and cultures
into a truly multiracial society.
Whatever divides us,
may much more unite.

We think of those who seek to break down barriers of
gender and sexuality –
to challenge stereotypical images,
to promote understanding and respect,
to overcome prejudice
and to uphold the rights of all.
Whatever divides us,
may much more unite.

In a world scarred by division,
where barriers are as much being erected as pulled down,
give wisdom and inspiration to all who work
to bring people together,
to promote harmony,
to build bridges,
to overcome whatever walls may keep us apart.
Whatever divides us,
may much more unite.
Amen.

12. Broken relationships, those experiencing

Lord of all,
hear our prayer for those experiencing problems
in their relationships.

We think of those experiencing tensions
in a relationship with a partner –
those who have drifted apart,
who have been hurt by thoughtless words
or careless actions,
whose partners have been unfaithful,
who have endured mental or physical cruelty.
Reach out to hold.
Reach out to help.

We think of those experiencing tensions
in a relationship with a child –
mothers coping with postnatal depression,
parents dealing with teenage angst and rebellion,
those finding it hard to let go of the apron strings,
those whose children have gone off the rails.
Reach out to hold.
Reach out to help.

We think of those experiencing tensions
in a relationship with a parent –
those who feel controlled or overprotected,
those struggling to live up to parental expectations,
those who have argued with parents and become estranged,
those who have been abused or mistreated by them.
Reach out to hold.
Reach out to help.

We think of those experiencing tensions
in a relationship with other family members –
those who have allowed molehills to become mountains,
resentments to fester,
disagreements to alienate,
discord to divide.
Reach out to hold.
Reach out to help.

We think of those experiencing tensions
in a relationship with a friend –
those whose friendship has been taken for granted,
whose trust has been abused,
whose relationship has been one-sided,
whose friends have failed to be there for them
when needed.
Reach out to hold.
Reach out to help.
Amen.

13. The bruised and broken

(*See also* Hurting, those who are)

Loving God,
we pray today for those who are bruised and broken by life.

We think of those who have suffered knocks in their
relationships,
their education,
their employment,
their health,
their finances –
all for whom life has dealt them blows
from which they are struggling to recover,
and that have left their confidence shaken,
their trust in others dented,
their hopes for the future undermined.
Heal their wounds
and give them new faith,
new conviction,
the ability to believe again in what life may hold.
Wherever lives are damaged,
make them whole.

We think of those who have been broken
by their experiences –
victims of abuse, rape, torture or other forms of violence;
those who have lost a child or another loved one
close to them;
those who have been broken by illness in body or mind;
soldiers and civilians who have been caught up in the
horrors of war;

those who have fallen victim to the lure of drugs
or alcohol;
those who have been cruelly deceived and betrayed.
Wherever lives are damaged,
make them whole.

We think of those who seek to bring healing
to the bruised and broken:
doctors, consultants, surgeons;
psychiatrists, counsellors and mental health nurses;
paramedics, nurses, physiotherapists;
care workers, chaplains and other clergy;
charities, support groups, aid agencies –
so many people in our world striving to bring comfort,
encouragement,
relief,
strength,
love
and hope.
Give them the resources they need,
wisdom to use them
and genuine compassion in all they do.
Wherever lives are damaged,
make them whole.
Amen.

14. Business leaders

Lord of life,
we think today of business leaders,
their decisions affecting the lives of so many.

We think of managers of global corporations
and companies –
of the investments that must be made or avoided,
marketing strategies developed and trends assessed,
the appointment of management and directors,
the hiring and firing of staff,
the shrinking or expanding of the business:
so many decisions that will shape not just their future
but that of countless others besides.
Give shrewdness.
Give guidance.

We think of national and regional enterprises –
high-street stores,
retail-park companies,
online businesses,
industrial-estate firms –
enterprises that provide employment for many,
bringing a sense of dignity, belonging and structure
to their lives.
Help them in the decisions they must make:
decisions that potentially could make or break them.
Give shrewdness.
Give guidance.

We think of those who run small businesses
and those who run their own,
many providing a vital service to the local community,
stimulating its economy,
catering to its needs
and providing a livelihood to local people.
Help them to plan sensibly for the future,
so that they may thrive.
Give shrewdness.
Give guidance.

To all in business give vision and initiative,
coupled with talent and integrity –
the ability to promote growth yet to maintain standards,
to care about staff and workers as much as profit
and to balance opportunity with responsibility.
Give shrewdness.
Give guidance.
Amen.

15. Cancer, sufferers from

(*See also* Chemotherapy and cancer treatment, those undergoing)

Lord of all,
hear our prayer today for all who are suffering from cancer.

We think of the shock felt at the time of diagnosis,
the uncertainty as to whether treatment will be successful,
the fear of what lies in store,
the anxiety shared by family and friends.
Give hope.
Give help.

We think of the challenge of coping with treatment,
as well as with the effects of the condition:
the nausea,
the pain,
the traipsing to and from hospital,
the anxious waiting for test results,
the financial implications,
the grim shadow that has fallen over life,
touching everything with a pall of uncertainty.
Give hope.
Give help.

We think of the worry faced by sufferers,
the fear that, if the worst comes to the worst and
treatment is unsuccessful,
they must face the heartbreak of saying goodbye
to loved ones,
in this life at least, never to see them again.
Give hope.
Give help.

We think of the challenge of carrying on despite all this –
of remaining cheerful and positive,
of attempting still to live a normal life,
of planning for the future while living as fully as possible
in the present.
Give hope.
Give help.

Grant skill, inspiration and guidance to all seeking a
cure for cancer,
so that generations to come may not live under its shadow
and sufferers today may have cause to look forward with
optimism to what may lie ahead.
Give hope.
Give help.
Amen.

16. Carers

Lord of all,
we pray today for carers:
those undertaking the vital but often overlooked work of
looking after loved ones,
caring for those unable to look after themselves,
often at significant cost to themselves,
their service entailing considerable personal sacrifice.
To all carers,
**give time, space and the resources they need
to care for themselves.**

Give them the strength they need when they feel weary,
patience in moments of frustration,
hope in times of despair,
strength when they feel exhausted,
comfort when they are sorrowful.
To all carers,
**give time, space and the resources they need
to care for themselves.**

Support them when their efforts are taken for granted,
or even meet with rejection;
renew them when they feel they have nothing left to give;
encourage them when they are frightened as to what the
future may hold,
uncertain as to whether they will be able to cope with
what's asked of them.
To all carers,
**give time, space and the resources they need
to care for themselves.**

Bring light and love into the lives of those they care for –
the knowledge that they are not alone,
not abandoned,
not seen simply as a disease, illness, problem,
but valued still as the people they continue to be –
and may offering that priceless gift bring constant
inspiration to carers in all they do.
To all carers,
**give time, space and the resources they need
to care for themselves.**

Grant that, as a society, we may recognise the vital
contribution made by carers,
and do all we can to support and enable them;
to assist their work
and ease the pressures they are under,
so that they, as much as those they care for,
may feel equipped,
valued,
and, above all, not alone in the situation
they continue to face.
To all carers,
**give time, space and the resources they need
to care for themselves.
Amen.**

17. Casualty departments

(*See also* Hospitals)

Lord of life,
hear our prayer for those who work in hospital A&E
departments,
their work so pressured,
so demanding.

We think of the responsibility of coping with a
never-ending stream of patients,
of reassuring anxious family and friends,
of having to meet often unrealistic government targets,
of needing to make speedy diagnoses,
of facing often drunk and abusive patients.
Give wisdom.
Give guidance.

We think of the challenge of having to deal with
contrasting needs and situations:
some injuries minor and swiftly patched up,
some illnesses obvious and easily treated,
but other conditions difficult to diagnose,
possibly trivial but potentially life threatening,
the outcome dependent on getting things right.
Give wisdom.
Give guidance.

We think of the stress involved in dealing with those
seriously, even critically, injured,
of battling to preserve life,
of working round the clock and against the clock
to provide care,
and of coming to terms with situations in which
nothing can be done,
breaking the news then to distraught partners and relatives.
Give wisdom.
Give guidance.

To doctors, nurses, surgeons,
and all involved in staffing such departments,
grant the strength, energy, skill, patience, compassion
and wisdom needed to do their job,
and to do it well.
Give wisdom.
Give guidance.
Amen.

18. Charities

(*See also* Aid agencies)

God of all,
we think today of charities, large and small.

We think of those that work in foreign countries,
seeking to improve the lot of the poor,
the hungry and the sick –
those in places fractured by war,
broken by natural disaster,
or scarred by injustice and exploitation.
Through their efforts,
bring progress and lasting change.

We think of those that strive to support the sick
in body or mind –
charities in the field of mental health,
dementia,
cancer,
heart disease,
multiple sclerosis,
and all kinds of other illnesses
that continue to challenge medicine
and blight lives.
Through their efforts,
bring progress and lasting change.

We think of those that support
and enable people with disabilities –
those born with congenital conditions,
those injured in accidents,
those who have lost limbs in battle,
those who have lost their sight or their hearing,
those who are paralysed.
Through their efforts,
bring progress and lasting change.

We pray for those that seek to preserve places of beauty,
to maintain buildings of historic interest,
to fund the arts,
or to further scientific research.
Through their efforts,
bring progress and lasting change.

We pray for those that seek to fund local projects,
to raise funds for specific needs,
to help deprived areas,
to support individuals in distress,
to improve the lot of residents.
Through their efforts,
bring progress and lasting change.

Grant to all charities integrity and vision –
the ability to raise the funds they require,
and above all to use them wisely,
so that they make a genuine difference
to society and our world.
Through their efforts,
bring progress and lasting change.
Amen.

19. Chemotherapy and cancer treatment, those undergoing

(*See also* Cancer, sufferers from; Health and healing)

Loving God,
we bring before you those suffering from cancer.

We think of those whose condition is treatable –
those who, through chemo, radiotherapy or surgery,
have every prospect of remission or recovery,
and who can look forward to life beyond the disease.
Give strength.
Give help.

We think of those with incurable but treatable cancer –
those who will need to undergo regular and often
demanding therapy,
but who can still hope for many months, even years of life,
and for whom the development of new drugs may mean
more time still
and perhaps even the possibility of a cure.
Give strength.
Give help.

We think of those with terminal cancer –
those who have been told they have months,
weeks or even days left to live,
and who must face the heartbreak of saying goodbye
to family and friends;
who must come to terms with the stark reality
of their mortality
and handle the imminent prospect of death,

with all the fears and uncertainty as to what
that will involve.
Give strength.
Give help.

We think of those newly diagnosed with cancer –
coming to terms with the shock as they attempt to digest
the news,
wrestling with its implications for themselves
and their family,
dealing with the confusion, fear, sadness, denial,
yet somehow attempting to live life as normally as possible.
Give strength.
Give help.

Guide those who will oversee the treatment
of cancer sufferers,
give wisdom to medical researchers and drug companies,
and reach out to all for whom cancer has cast a shadow
over their lives –
patients, loved ones, friends –
granting them the strength to get through,
whatever it may bring.
Give strength.
Give help.
Amen.

20. Children leaving home

(*See also* Young people)

Lord God,
we pray for children who are leaving home,
and for their families.

We think of young people leaving for college and
university,
filled with a mixture of excitement and trepidation –
looking forward on the one hand to flexing their wings
and asserting their independence,
but nervous also at the prospect of coping by themselves,
away from the security of family and friends;
of making ends meet;
of dealing with their studies.
Bring reassurance in the present.
Grant joy in the future.

We think of young people moving away to start a new job,
to get married and settle down,
or simply to see the world,
again caught between a mixture of anticipation
and uncertainty –
enthusiastic about starting a new chapter
but a little unsure about what the next page might bring.
Bring reassurance in the present.
Grant joy in the future.

We pray for parents and siblings of those leaving home,
struggling perhaps to adjust to an empty bed
or room in the house,
a vacant place at the table
and an aching space in the heart –
the pain of separation feeling at first like a bereavement.
Help them to let go and to adjust to a new chapter
in life for them all.
Bring reassurance in the present.
Grant joy in the future.

We think of children who have run away from home –
those who have lost contact with their family;
those who have ended up living on the streets or in hostels;
those for whom a great adventure
has turned into a nightmare.
Bring reassurance in the present.
Grant joy in the future.

Watch over all young people who have left home.
Give them guidance,
wisdom,
protection,
support
and fulfilment.
Help them and their families in dealing with change,
and may the end of one stage of life lead on to exciting
new beginnings.
Bring reassurance in the present.
Bring joy in the future.
Amen.

21. Confidence in themselves, those lacking

Lord God,
hear our prayer today for those who lack confidence
in themselves;
all who question their own worth.

We think of those who put themselves down because of
their looks,
their body,
their job,
their income,
or their academic performance or abilities.
Whoever they may be,
give to all a proper sense of worth.

We think of those who are shy,
self-conscious,
socially awkward,
easily embarrassed –
all who feel uncomfortable and unsure of themselves
in company.
Whoever they may be,
give to all a proper sense of worth.

We think of those who undervalue themselves due to
illness or disability,
who feel themselves to be a shadow
of what they once were,
who consider themselves a burden to others,
who feel less than a whole person.
Whoever they may be,
give to all a proper sense of worth.

We think of those who have been made to feel small by
others –
bullied,
put down,
teased,
persecuted –
their self-esteem gradually eroded by repeated assault.
Whoever they may be,
give to all a proper sense of worth.

We think of those whose worth is casually dismissed –
their value overlooked on account of their mistakes,
their past,
their background
or their class –
their importance measured in terms of income,
prospects,
breeding
or influence.
Whoever they may be,
give to all a proper sense of worth.
Amen.

22. Conservation

(*See also* Animal welfare; The environment)

God of all,
hear our prayer for those involved in the work of
conservation.

We think of those in other countries striving to safeguard
endangered species,
clamping down on the sale of elephant and rhino horn,
preventing poaching,
preserving habitats,
working, if possible, to safeguard the wonderful
biodiversity of this planet.
You have given us a wonderful world.
Help us to protect it for future generations to enjoy.

We think of those who seek to preserve the ecosystems
of the oceans –
to save whales from hunting,
fish stocks from over-exploitation,
coral reefs from pollution,
turtles from extinction.
You have given us a wonderful world.
Help us to protect it for future generations to enjoy.

We think of those who campaign to save rainforests,
who take on logging and clearcutting companies,
who plant new woodlands,
who combat the effects of acid rain –
each seeking to preserve a resource so vital
for this world's ecology.
You have given us a wonderful world.
Help us to protect it for future generations to enjoy.

We think of those who protect birdlife –
who establish reserves,
defend vulnerable species from persecution,
monitor populations
and aim to raise public awareness of their needs.
You have given us a wonderful world.
Help us to protect it for future generations to enjoy.

We think of those who work to maintain the countryside,
to preserve the unique character of our land,
to safeguard flora and fauna,
to ensure that places of natural beauty
are not lost to development
but are open instead to us all.
You have given us a wonderful world.
Help us to protect it for future generations to enjoy.
Amen.

23.   Crime, victims of

Loving God,
we pray today for all who have been victims of crime.

We think of those who have been burgled –
left feeling that their home
has been violated;
mourning the loss, perhaps, of sentimental items
that can never be replaced;
no longer feeling able to sleep at night;
fearful for their own safety or that of loved ones.
To all victims of crime,
give help to come to terms with their experience.

We think of those mugged or attacked in the street –
of elderly people no longer feeling safe
to leave their homes,
young people terrified of violent gangs,
residents in estates where the rule of law has been replaced
by the law of the jungle.
To all victims of crime,
give help to come to terms with their experience.

We think of those who have been abused as children,
their lives left blighted by memories
of what they went through,
many never having plucked up the courage
to share them with anyone,
some still wrestling years later with the resulting
psychological damage.
To all victims of crime,
give help to come to terms with their experience.

We think of victims of rape,
equally traumatised by what they have faced,
their view of the opposite sex sometimes changed for ever,
their relationships deeply affected,
their sense of self-worth undermined.
To all victims of crime,
give help to come to terms with their experience.

We think of victims of drunk-driving
and of hit-and-run accidents –
men and women deprived of a partner,
parents robbed of a child,
children of a mother and father,
brothers and sisters mourning a sibling,
friends grieving for one they've lost,
each struggling to come to terms with their bereavement –
the knowledge that it should never have happened,
and that the punishment can never erase the crime,
assuming the perpetrator is brought to justice.
To all victims of crime,
give help to come to terms with their experience.

We think of victims of scams –
those caught out by door-to-door callers,
by rip-off advertisements or bogus correspondence,
by online hackers or conmen,
some having life savings stolen,
all experiencing huge trauma and substantial upheaval.
To all victims of crime,
give help to come to terms with their experience.
Amen.

24. The deaf and aurally impaired

Lord of all,
we think today of those who are hard of hearing;
the many people who are denied enjoyment of the sounds
we take for granted.

We think of those who do not hear as well as they used to –
those who struggle to follow a conversation,
feeling isolated in a crowd;
those who can no longer hear the song of birds,
or other natural sounds in the world around them,
as they once did;
those who find music distorted
when they try to listen to it;
those who are treated as slow or stupid
on account of their growing deafness.
To all who struggle to hear,
give help to cope.

We think of those who have lost their hearing completely
or who were born deaf;
those who, throughout their life, have had to communicate
via lip reading or sign language,
and those who have had to learn such skills as their
condition has worsened;
those who have to live
in a world of silence.
To all who struggle to hear,
give help to cope.

We think of those whose speech has been affected
by their deafness –
who struggle to make themselves understood as a result of it,
who feel awkward and even stupid
in their attempts to communicate,
who keep silent rather than risk embarrassing themselves.
To all who struggle to hear,
give help to cope.

We think of those given a diagnosis of progressive deafness,
having to reconcile themselves to an increasingly
soundless world,
wrestling with a multitude of fears as to whether
they'll be able to cope,
dreading the future and panicking every time
they cannot catch what's being said.
To all who struggle to hear,
give help to cope.

We think of doctors, consultants, specialists and surgeons
who treat deafness –
who design and fit hearing aids,
who research into its causes,
who seek to discover new treatments,
who offer help and support to those whose hearing has
failed or is failing.
To all who struggle to hear,
give help to cope.
Amen.

25. Dementia

(See also The elderly; Nursing/residential care homes)

Loving God,
we bring before you the trauma of dementia,
and all those who wrestle with it.

We think of those who have just received a diagnosis
and who are coming to terms with what it means:
the growing loss of their mind and faculties,
their relationships and independence,
their sense of who and what they are.
In all they face,
be with them.

We pray for those in whom the disease
has started to progress,
causing growing confusion,
anxiety,
frustration
and fear.
In all they face,
be with them.

We pray for those in whom dementia
has taken hold completely –
those locked now in a world of the past,
often confined to a hospital or nursing home,
unable to recognise loved ones and friends,
unable equally to take in what's going on around them
for more than a moment.
In all they face,
be with them.

We pray for the families of those with dementia,
seeking to care for them despite it sometimes feeling they
are living with a stranger,
despite their loved one speaking and acting in ways that
can feel hurtful.
And we pray for those who seek to offer help
and support to them,
to give moments of respite from their daily responsibilities.
In all they face,
be with them.

We think of doctors, nurses, care workers,
attempting to offer whatever assistance they can,
to help bear the burden of caring,
and to make the patient as comfortable
and content as possible.
In all they face,
be with them.

We think of those working on treatments for Alzheimer's
and other forms of dementia –
those investigating its causes,
those developing new drugs for its treatment,
those conducting pioneering research
and those undergoing trials,
all hoping to help develop a cure
for this cruellest of diseases.
In all they face,
be with them.
Amen.

26. The depressed

God of love,
we bring before you those wrestling with depression –
all for whom life has become dark,
no longer a pleasure but a burden,
a black hole from which there seems to be no escape.
Lift their despair,
and bring joy and hope once more.

We think of those depressed by the events of life,
overwhelmed, perhaps, by the loss of a job,
a loved one,
a relationship,
a dream –
struggling to come to terms
with their changed circumstances,
everything that had shone so brightly
suddenly cast into shadow.
Lift their despair,
and bring joy and hope once more.

We think of those who are clinically depressed –
those for whom life has felt empty for weeks,
months,
even years,
each day seeming as meaningless as the next one,
greeted with the same listlessness,
disinterest and heaviness of heart.
Lift their despair,
and bring joy and hope once more.

We think of those experiencing the dark night of the soul,
even their faith no longer able to lift their spirits,
their cries to you for help seeming to fall on deaf ears,
their convictions no longer speaking as they once did,
their commitment feeling more apparent than real.
Lift their despair,
and bring joy and hope once more.

We think of those who have been driven to the end
of their tether,
who yearn for the oblivion of death,
who have turned to drugs and alcohol in their quest
to fill the void,
who have contemplated suicide,
who perhaps even now are on the verge
of taking that final step.
Lift their despair,
and bring joy and hope once more.

We think of those who attempt to help and support
the depressed –
friends, family, doctors, counsellors.
Give them wisdom, empathy, patience, compassion,
and, above all, the ability to listen without judging,
without expecting instant results,
but ready simply to be there alongside the depressed
in their time of need.
Lift their despair,
and bring joy and hope once more.
Amen.

27. Deprivation

(*See also* The hungry; Injustice; The poor and needy;
The poorly paid; Social justice; The underpaid)

Lord of all,
hear our prayer for the deprived of our world,
whether in body, mind or spirit.

We think of those who are deprived materially –
people of the so-called Third World –
so many of them living with the daily reality of hunger,
denied the basics we take for granted;
disease, hardship and poverty a simple fact of life.
For all in such need,
give hope and help.

We think of those in our own country living at or below
the poverty line;
of those who sleep rough on the streets;
of those who cannot find work and shelter;
of all who feel they are denied a stake in society
and a future to look forward to.
For all in such need,
give hope and help.

We think of those denied a voice,
denied freedom,
denied justice,
denied opportunity.
For all in such need,
give hope and help.

We think of those deprived emotionally –
those who lack love,
lack purpose,
lack hope,
lack joy –
people who may seem to have everything
yet who in fact have nothing.
For all in such need,
give hope and help.

We think of those deprived spiritually –
those who are no longer moved by the wonder
of the universe;
who no longer catch their breath at sights and sounds
in awe and wonder;
who no longer have faith in anything beyond themselves.
For all in such need,
give hope and help.
Amen.

28. Diagnosis, those awaiting or receiving

(*See also* GPs; Health and healing; Hospitals)

Loving God,
we pray for those awaiting the results
of medical investigations,
fearful of what the diagnosis might be.

We think of those who have been ill for some time,
their symptoms developing,
their condition giving ever greater cause for concern –
many having a good idea of what may be wrong with them,
but waiting for confirmation
and dreading the consequences.
Bring healing.
Bring wholeness.

We think of those for whom diagnoses
come as a sudden shock –
those who had little if any idea that something was wrong
until a routine examination,
precautionary blood test,
mammogram or x-ray
highlighted unexpected problems,
a disease requiring urgent attention.
Bring healing.
Bring wholeness.

We think of those whose diagnosis will mean major surgery;
those for whom it will involve long and demanding
drug treatment;
those who will have to deal with the impact of radiotherapy;
those who must get used to living with chronic,
often painful conditions;

those who face the prospect of life in a wheelchair
or a slow decline in their faculties;
and those who are told they have a terminal illness,
their world turned upside down in a moment.
Bring healing.
Bring wholeness.

We think of those for whom the diagnosis will be good news:
a complete all-clear, perhaps,
tests coming back negative,
or their condition proving less serious,
less frightening than they imagined.
We think of their joy and relief,
together with that of their family and friends,
but we think also of the trauma,
the worry,
the dismay
and the challenge faced by so many
for whom a diagnosis confirms all that they fear.
Bring healing.
Bring wholeness.

Guide GPs and consultants –
all who must share news good and bad with their patients.
Give them sensitivity, compassion, wisdom –
the ability to find the best words to say,
to offer the best treatment,
to comfort and encourage,
and to give hope wherever possible.
And grant continued progress in research,
that diagnoses which once were feared will be feared no more.
Bring healing.
Bring wholeness.
Amen.

29. The disillusioned

Lord God,
hear our prayer for those disillusioned by life.

We think of those in war-torn or impoverished countries –
people who have put their faith in politicians,
world leaders
and international goodwill,
only to have their hopes shattered by subsequent events;
violence, disease, hunger and poverty continuing
to stalk their land.
Give reason to trust;
reason to look forward again.

We think of those who have had the prospect of change
held out to them,
only to be let down,
promises having been broken,
help having proven inadequate,
expediency having got in the way of principle,
such that they no longer know who or what to believe,
and no longer dare hope for the future.
Give reason to trust;
reason to look forward again.

We think of those who have put their trust in individuals –
family,
friends,
colleagues,
role models –
only to be left feeling betrayed,
hurt,
used,

no longer having any faith in human nature
or feeling able to believe in people as they once did.
Give reason to trust;
reason to look forward again.

We think of those who have lost faith in their leaders –
disillusioned by politics,
feeling unrepresented,
let down by empty promises,
dismayed by party infighting or intransigence,
disheartened by what they see as careerism rather than
principled conviction –
governments failing to tackle the real issues of the day.
Give reason to trust;
reason to look forward again.

We think finally of those who have lost faith in you –
those overwhelmed by tragedy;
those whose prayers seem unanswered;
those struggling to reconcile doubts and questions
with established doctrine;
those disillusioned by the actions of your followers;
those for whom religion seems irrelevant,
divorced from daily life.
Give reason to trust;
reason to look forward again.

Reach out to all whose trust has been undermined,
whose faith in others has proven misjudged,
whose belief in the future has been eroded,
who no longer feel able to hope.
Give reason to trust;
reason to look forward again.
Amen.

30. Drought

(*See also* Natural disaster, those overwhelmed by)

Lord of all,
hear our prayer for those in countries suffering from
drought.

We think of those whose lands are parched and barren,
whose livelihoods have been destroyed,
whose crops have failed,
and who now face hunger,
thirst
and the prospect of starvation.
Bring hope.
Bring change.

We think of the governments of the prosperous nations
of this world –
those with the resources to reach out and help,
to offer genuine support,
meaningful programmes of aid –
and we think also of charities and voluntary organisations,
striving to bring immediate assistance coupled with
long-term transformation.
Bring hope.
Bring change.

We think of the challenge posed by climate change,
the growing problems faced by many nations
as weather patterns alter,
as rains fail to come,
as the threat of prolonged drought
becomes ever more pressing.
Bring hope.
Bring change.

Stir the hearts of people everywhere to respond to those less fortunate than themselves.
Challenge those most able to help to do what they can, and give to all directly affected by drought the resources they need somehow to adapt,
to adjust
and to help themselves.
Bring hope.
Bring change.
Amen.

31. Drug addicts

(*See also* Alcoholics)

Loving God,
hear our prayer today for those addicted to drugs.

We think of those who experiment with soft drugs,
thinking they can use them purely for recreation
and that they will not lead to anything else,
but then finding themselves mentally
if not physically dependent,
increasingly tempted to try something stronger.
To all seeking solace, pleasure or escape in drugs,
give true fulfilment.

We think of those who experiment with
so-called legal highs,
believing them to be safe yet some users suffering
untold damage,
and we think of the heartbreak of those who have lost
loved ones to such drugs,
lives snuffed out in a moment.
Give to all a greater awareness of the risks involved,
the dangers to which they are exposing themselves.
To all seeking solace, pleasure or escape in drugs,
give true fulfilment.

We think of young people being offered drugs at school,
college,
university –
perhaps believing they can take them as a one-off,
only to find themselves sucked into the nightmare world
of drug dependency.
To all seeking solace, pleasure or escape in drugs,
give true fulfilment.

We think of those who have become addicted
to hard drugs –
those who cannot get through the day without a fix,
who need to beg or steal to fund their habit,
who have lost home, livelihood, partner or self-respect
due to the depths into which their addiction
has brought them.
To all seeking solace, pleasure or escape in drugs,
give true fulfilment.

We think finally of those who seek to treat addiction,
who deal with its consequences,
who nurse addicts or seek to rehabilitate them,
who seek to support family or friends
who have become users
or who legislate concerning drugs.
Grant them patience, compassion, empathy and wisdom,
that they may truly be able to offer hope,
help
and new beginnings.
To all seeking solace, pleasure or escape in drugs,
give true fulfilment.
Amen.

32. The elderly

(*See also* Dementia; Nursing/residential care homes)

God of all,
we bring before you today the elderly.

We think of those for whom age has brought opportunities
as well as challenges:
those who feel liberated by retirement,
who find they have extra time to offer to others –
to grandchildren and family,
to voluntary work or local organisations,
to friends and colleagues –
or perhaps, for the first time, to themselves
and their partners,
living life in a way that simply was not possible before.
In every chapter of life,
give strength, support, hope and joy.

We think of those for whom advancing years
have brought health problems:
increasing frailty,
the aches and pains of arthritis,
the burden of chronic illness,
the onset of cancer or other life-threatening conditions –
so much that undermines their quality of life
and that brings with it not just frustration and worry,
but also the fear of being a burden to others.
In every chapter of life,
give strength, support, hope and joy.

We think of those who are facing the prospect of dementia,
anxious and confused,
terrified by the thought of losing their mind
and their dignity;
and we think also of their loved ones,
struggling to cope with the implications of such a diagnosis
and with the likelihood of losing their loved one
even while they are yet alive.
In every chapter of life,
give strength, support, hope and joy.

We think of those who have lost a partner, brother or sister,
a close friend or colleague,
suddenly faced with the challenge of coping on their own,
devoid of the love and companionship they have long
taken for granted.
In every chapter of life,
give strength, support, hope and joy.

Reach out to all facing old age.
Give comfort in time of loss,
support through illness,
peace in moments of anxiety,
strength in weakness
and hope in despair.
And to those who seek to respond to the needs
of the elderly,
give guidance, patience, empathy and compassion,
so that they may give support where and when
it is needed most.
In every chapter of life,
give strength, support, hope and joy.
Amen.

33. The environment

(*See also* Animal welfare; Conservation)

Lord of all,
we think today of our environment
and of those who seek to protect it for future generations.

We think of individuals striving to live more responsibly –
recycling whatever they can,
purchasing environmentally friendly products
where possible,
cutting down on waste,
considering where and how they drive –
doing everything in their power
to reduce their ecological footprint.
Help all to understand better what steps they can take
and to act upon them.
Teach us today
to think of tomorrow.

We think of environmental groups and campaigners:
those who monitor the health of our planet
and our impact upon it;
who seek to promote wider awareness of ecological issues;
who stand up for green policies against vested interest
and corporate greed.
Give them a platform to speak
and the ability to make a real and lasting difference.
Teach us today
to think of tomorrow.

We think of governments, delegates and politicians –
those who must strike a balance between environmental
and economic concerns,
conservation and development;
safeguarding life itself as opposed merely to standards
of living.
Give them wisdom and courage in the choices
they must make –
pragmatism where necessary
but never at the cost of a wider idealism.
May they consider not just the present generation,
but those to follow;
not just short-term gain,
but long-term sustainability.
Teach us today
to think of tomorrow.

We think of meteorologists who study the climate,
scientists who explore the delicate balance of life,
researchers who collect and interpret data –
all who help us to gauge the health of this world
and what might threaten it.
Help them to outline the steps needed
to promote life on earth,
not just for today
but for tomorrow and far beyond.
Teach us today
to think of tomorrow.
Amen.

34. The exploited and abused

(*See also* Abuse, victims of; Pornography)

Loving God,
hear our prayer for those who are exploited or abused,
those whose humanity is wantonly demeaned,
denied or degraded.

We think of victims of modern slavery.
Grant help.
Grant hope.

We think of those trafficked for sex.
Grant help.
Grant hope.

We think of those trapped in a life of prostitution.
Grant help.
Grant hope.

We think of victims of rape or sexual assault.
Grant help.
Grant hope.

We think of battered wives and victims of emotional abuse.
Grant help.
Grant hope.

We think of those haunted by stalkers.
Grant help.
Grant hope.

We think of those who have been abused as children.
Grant help.
Grant hope.

We think of those who are wrongly imprisoned
or held captive.
Grant help.
Grant hope.

We think of victims of torture.
Grant help.
Grant hope.

We think of those persecuted on account of their faith,
race,
sex
or gender.
Grant help.
Grant hope.

Reach out, we pray, to all who are abused,
all who are exploited,
all who are treated as less than human.
Grant help.
Grant hope.
Amen.

35. Extremism

(*See also* Terrorism)

Lord God,
we pray today for our world,
haunted by the spectre of extremism.

We pray for our Intelligence services –
those in the front line of monitoring suspicious activity,
infiltrating terror cells,
tracking suspects,
thwarting plots,
often at great risk to themselves.
Wherever extremism rears its head,
may moderation and justice prevail.

We think of police,
ambulance crews,
fire services
and hospital staff –
those trained to deal with a terrorist incident,
potentially having to cope with mass casualties
in the event of an attack.
Wherever extremism rears its head,
may moderation and justice prevail.

We think of the victims of terrorism –
those who have been killed in atrocities;
those who have been maimed,
often suffering life-changing injuries;
those who have lost loved ones,
their lives never the same again;
those who have been traumatised by the sights and sounds
they've witnessed,
unable to get them out of their minds.
Wherever extremism rears its head,
may moderation and justice prevail.

We think of extremists themselves –
those who have lost sight of their common humanity;
who have allowed political and religious ideology
to poison their minds,
shutting out the true principles of their faith;
those who have turned what, at times,
are legitimate grievances
into wholly illegitimate and indiscriminate murder.
Help them to see that religion without love is no faith at all,
and that any movement based on hate can ultimately only
end up hateful . . .
and hated.
Wherever extremism rears its head,
may moderation and justice prevail.
Amen.

36. Factories and industry

(See also An industrial dispute)

Lord of all,
we pray today for factories and industry,
and for all those employed within these.

We think of those on production lines,
their work often dull and repetitive,
their jobs sometimes feeling under threat due to
increasing automation,
their wages driven down by foreign competition,
their future at times feeling insecure.
To all in such positions,
grant help to give their best.

We think of those in positions of responsibility –
managers and directors,
supervisors and team leaders,
accounts departments, sales and marketing teams,
and other office staff –
those who hire and fire,
who deal with personnel and their problems,
who seek to maximise efficiency or to promote sales,
who contribute to the day-to-day running of affairs.
To all in such positions,
grant help to give their best.

We think of support staff –
stock controllers,
warehouse operatives,
drivers,
engineers,
technicians,
canteen workers –
all who are part of the wider structure of a business.
To all in such positions,
grant help to give their best.

We think of those responsible for maintaining standards,
whether in the workplace or in terms of what is produced –
health and safety officials,
quality-control staff,
trade unions and employee representatives,
auditors and accountants,
environmental officers.
To all in such positions,
grant help to give their best.

Help all involved in our factories and industry
to work together,
so that the companies they are part of may grow
and move forward,
responding to the challenge of changing times,
and offering meaningful employment and lasting security
for years to come.
To all in such positions,
grant help to give their best.
Amen.

37. Failure, those who feel they are

Lord God,
hear our prayer for those who feel they are a failure.

We think of those who feel they have failed others –
who believe they have let down loved ones,
betrayed friendships,
disappointed colleagues.
Whatever the mistakes of the past,
help them to embrace the future.

We think of those who feel they have failed in life –
to fulfil their potential,
to succeed academically or in work,
to build happy relationships,
to be as good a parent as they intended,
to find the happiness and fulfilment they crave.
Whatever the mistakes of the past,
help them to embrace the future.

We think of those who feel they have failed you –
who feel burdened by a weight of guilt,
by their lack of commitment,
by an inability to live as they want to,
by promises made and broken,
or by a sense of their many faults and weaknesses.
Whatever the mistakes of the past,
help them to embrace the future.

To all who feel they have failed
or who deem themselves to be a failure,
give the assurance that what's done is done,
that there is always an opportunity for new beginnings,
that they can put tomorrow behind them and start afresh.
Whatever the mistakes of the past,
help them to embrace the future.
Amen.

38. Farmers

(See also Animal welfare)

God of all,
we bring to you today all who live and work on the land.

We think of the particular pressures farmers and their
families face:
the early mornings,
the long hours,
the working in all winds and weathers,
the daily list of chores and duties.
Give help.
Give guidance.

We think of the challenge farmers face in adjusting to
changing times:
the need to weigh up markets and decide whether to focus
on crops or livestock,
or a combination of the two –
their livelihood potentially depending on reaching
the right decision.
Give help.
Give guidance.

We think of the difficulty farmers experience in negotiating
a fair price for their products –
the constant attempts by supermarkets and retailers
to drive down prices,
the financial pressure this creates,
the difficulties in making ends meet.
Give help.
Give guidance.

We think of the threat of disease and pests,
flood or drought,
each potentially devastating,
yet we think also of the need to farm responsibly,
to minimise the use of antibiotics, pesticides,
weed killers and artificial fertilisers,
to retain the character of the countryside,
and to protect the environment wherever possible.
Give help.
Give guidance.

We think of farmers who have been driven to despair
by the demands of their job,
even to the point of suicide.
And we think of those who are struggling
to survive financially,
who have sold up or gone bankrupt,
whose land has been turned over to housing,
golf courses or retail developments.
Give help.
Give guidance.

To all farmers,
grant support,
encouragement
and vision,
so that they may farm wisely and well
and feel that there is a purpose
and a future
in all they do.
Give help.
Give guidance.
Amen.

39. Firefighters

Lord God,
hear our prayer for those who serve as firefighters.

We think of those who serve full time in the fire brigade,
and of those who serve part time,
holding down other jobs
but responding to the call when needed.
In all they do,
protect them.

We reflect on their courage, skill and dedication,
and of their willingness if necessary to put the safety
of others before their own.
In all they do,
protect them.

We think of those who have to tackle particularly
dangerous situations:
premises burning out of control,
buildings at risk of collapse,
or with the added perils of a possible explosion,
release of toxic chemicals,
or radioactive contamination.
In all they do,
protect them.

We think of those who train firefighters,
who manage fire stations,
who command a crew
or who drive the engines.
In all they do,
protect them.

We entrust to you all those we rely on in the event of fire,
and ask for them guidance,
skill,
courage
and safety.
In all they do,
protect them.
Amen.

40. Fishermen and sailors

(*See also* Lifeboat and air-sea rescue crews)

Loving God,
we think of those who spend time in their work or leisure
on the sea.

We think especially of fishermen,
their work often difficult and dangerous,
involving hours on stormy waters,
the threat of their boat capsizing
or of crew being swept overboard –
numerous occasions when they need to gauge
when it is safe to put out
and when it is wiser to remain in harbour.
Whatever they may face,
grant them protection.

We think of those in the Navy,
sailors serving in battleships, aircraft carriers,
submarines and other vessels,
often spending weeks and even months away
from family and home;
and we think particularly of those
who have to face active service –
the danger of being attacked
in addition to the perils of the sea.
Whatever they may face,
grant them protection.

We think of those on cruise liners, ferries and lifeboats,
their crew in different ways responsible for others
as well as themselves,
entrusted with ensuring the safety of passengers
or with striving to save those in trouble on the water.
Whatever they may face,
grant them protection.

We think of those on container ships,
oil tankers and merchant vessels,
vital to trade across the world,
integral to modern-day economies,
yet once again potentially vulnerable to the vagaries
of the weather
and uncertainties of the ocean.
Whatever they may face,
grant them protection.

We think of those who take to the sea for pleasure,
in yachts, launches, speedboats, jet skis and the like –
those for whom the sea presents a thrill,
challenge and pleasure,
but for whom it can also so easily become a threat
to their lives,
a bringer of death.
Whatever they may face,
grant them protection.

To all who spend time on the water,
give guidance, skill and discretion.
And wherever they venture,
may they return safely once more to shore.
Whatever they may face,
grant them protection.
Amen.

41. Floods, those overwhelmed by

(*See also* Natural disaster, those overwhelmed by)

(*Check and adjust wording as necessary to the specific situation*)

God of all,
we remember today those who have been caught up
in recent floods.

We think of those who have lost their lives,
people trapped in their homes or vehicles,
or swept away by the current.
We pray for those who mourn them,
their lives suddenly deluged with shock and sorrow.
And we think also of those who are still in danger,
waiting for rescue as the waters rise.
Reach out to help.
Reach out to save.

We think of those whose homes have been swamped,
furnishings and possessions left useless,
buildings needing weeks, months, even years before they
can be habitable again,
so much chaos and confusion left to deal with.
We pause for a moment to consider the heartbreak and
stress so many are going through.

Pause for silent reflection

Reach out to help.
Reach out to save.

We think of businesses forced to close,
farms under water and livestock drowned,
bridges destroyed and roads undermined,
communities cut off,
livelihoods threatened.
Reach out to help.
Reach out to save.

We think of those entrusted with overseeing flood defences
and prevention.
Guide them in their planning and decisions,
as they seek, with limited resources,
to adjust to a changing climate,
so that damage may be prevented where possible,
danger averted
and, above all, lives saved.
Reach out to help.
Reach out to save.
Amen.

42. Governments and world leaders

(See also World leaders)

Lord of all,
we think today of world leaders,
of politicians and governments,
of local councillors and authorities –
all who take decisions, large or small,
that will shape the lives of others.
Guide their deliberations,
**and grant them wisdom, vision and integrity
in all they do.**

Though some will not agree with their decisions,
and others will directly oppose them,
help leaders to listen to all points of view
and to pursue what they genuinely believe
to be in the interests of all
rather than narrow party or self-interest.
Guide their deliberations,
**and grant them wisdom, vision and integrity
in all they do.**

We think of the difficulties leaders face:
the challenge of balancing principle with pragmatism;
of seeking to please all rather than just some;
of trying to allocate limited resources
to seemingly endless needs;
of living under constant public scrutiny.
Guide their deliberations,
**and grant them wisdom, vision and integrity
in all they do.**

Help us to give leaders the respect they are due
but also to hold them to account;
to appreciate their efforts
but also to challenge them where necessary;
to listen to what they have to say
but to do what we can to ensure they listen equally
to those they represent,
so that the business of government
may truly be *of* the people,
for the people.
Guide their deliberations,
and grant them wisdom, vision and integrity
in all they do.
Amen.

43. GPs

(*See also* Diagnosis, those awaiting or receiving; Health and healing)

Lord of all,
hear our prayer for those who serve as GPs.

We think of the increasing pressures they are under –
the challenge they face of balancing increasing patient
numbers with limited time
and shrinking resources;
the demands of an ever more unrealistic workload
and the inevitable sense of frustration this leads to.
In all the challenges doctors face,
encourage and equip them.

We think of the pressures of daily practice:
of staying up to date with latest developments
in medicine and understanding;
of striving not to miss an important symptom
and make a wrong diagnosis;
of breaking bad news to patients;
of dealing with those who are awkward or aggressive.
In all the challenges doctors face,
encourage and equip them.

We think of those training as GPs –
the long years of study and preparation,
the demanding hours as a junior doctor,
the stress of exams and assessment,
and the need to ensure that lessons are well learnt.
In all the challenges doctors face,
encourage and equip them.

Grant help to all GPs,
and give them the resources, skill, time and wisdom
they need to do their job
and to do it well.
In all the challenges doctors face,
encourage and equip them.
Amen.

44. Health and healing

(See also Arthritis; Cancer, sufferers from; Casualty
departments; Chemotherapy and cancer treatment, those
undergoing; Dementia; Diagnosis, those awaiting or
receiving; GPs; Hospices and the terminally ill; Hospitals;
Mental illness, those wrestling with; The National Health
Service; Nurses; Paralysis; The physically disabled; Surgeons)

Loving God,
hear our prayer for those who are sick
and those who seek to treat them.

We think of those faced by sudden ill health,
those wrestling with long-term disease,
those suffering from disabling conditions of body
and mind,
those undergoing painful or debilitating treatment
or surgery,
those coming to terms with terminal illness.
In body, mind and spirit,
bring healing,
bring wholeness.

Grant to all who are sick, your help and strength,
peace and reassurance,
comfort and support,
courage and hope.
In body, mind and spirit,
bring healing,
bring wholeness.

We pray for those who work to bring healing:
consultants and surgeons,
GPs and hospital doctors,
nurses and medical staff,
osteopaths and chiropractors,
those practising in alternative medicine,
those seeking to bring spiritual healing.
In body, mind and spirit,
bring healing,
bring wholeness.

To all who strive to bring health,
give wisdom,
guidance,
inspiration,
compassion –
the ability to foster inner wholeness and lasting recovery.
In body, mind and spirit,
bring healing,
bring wholeness.
Amen.

45. The homeless

(See also Refugees)

Loving God,
hear our prayer for the homeless.

We think of those living as refugees,
driven from their homes by war and violence,
forced to take up shelter in makeshift camps,
lacking even the most basic resources,
devoid of sanitation and rife with disease.
Bring hope.
Bring shelter.

We think of the sense of loss, hopelessness and fear
refugees must feel,
their fate dependent on warring factions,
aid convoys
and international goodwill.
Bring hope.
Bring shelter.

We think of the homeless in our own country –
vagrants who sleep rough on the streets,
those in hostels or temporary accommodation,
those brought low by drug or alcohol abuse who have
dropped out of society.
And we think also of young people who have run away
from home;
of those whose homes have been repossessed
because they couldn't pay the rent or keep up with mortgage;
and of those living with family or friends
after having split up with a partner.
Bring hope.
Bring shelter.

We think of those who seek to respond to the plight
of the homeless –
governments and charities,
social workers and voluntary organisations –
all who seek to address its causes,
to meet the ever-increasing demand for housing,
to provide a roof over people's heads,
to give all somewhere to call home.
Bring hope.
Bring shelter.
Amen.

46. Homophobia

God of all,
we pray for victims of homophobia
and for all who face prejudice, even persecution,
on account of their sexuality.

We think of members of the gay community,
cruelly treated and discriminated against in the past,
and still dismissed by some as 'deviants' or 'perverts',
regarded as 'sick',
or even 'sinful',
on account of their sexual orientation.
Challenge the prejudice that continues to lurk in society,
prosper the efforts of those who work to break it down,
and help those who are attracted by their own sex
to hold their heads up high.
Where prejudice divides,
may love unite.

We think of those in the wider LGBT community –
all whose lives have been blighted across the years by
ridicule,
mistrust,
antagonism
and harassment,
driving many to the edge of despair,
all because they do not conform to what society
deems 'straight'.
Help them not just to find acceptance
but to feel accepted instead of judged, mocked or reviled.
Where prejudice divides,
may love unite.

We think of the many people today
who remain homophobic,
closed to those of different sexual orientations,
many basing such attitudes on religious convictions
when they ought to know better than to judge others.
We think of those who still abuse or persecute people on
account of their sexuality,
masking their own insecurities by lashing out
at what they fear or do not understand.
Challenge such bigotry, preconceptions and immaturity,
and help all to live together in harmony and
understanding.
Where prejudice divides,
may love unite.
Amen.

47.   Hospices and the terminally ill

(*See also* Hospitals; The sick and suffering)

Loving God,
hear our prayer for the work of hospices
and all those who receive care and treatment within them.

We think of patients going in for respite care,
not yet at the end of their lives,
but their loved ones needing a break from looking after them,
time to recharge their batteries and enjoy a few moments
for themselves.
Grant them rest and refreshment.
Give strength.
Give succour.

We think of patients going in to enjoy creative activities –
painting and drawing,
craftwork,
knitting,
singing,
card making,
and a host of other things designed to enhance their
quality of life,
to boost self-confidence and esteem,
and to lift anxiety.
Give strength.
Give succour.

We think of patients who are dying or close to death –
dependent on palliative care to ease their pain
and to keep them as comfortable as possible;
seeking comfort and reassurance,
support for themselves and their loved ones,
help and strength as they enter the unknown.
Give strength.
Give succour.

We think of the nurses and carers who staff hospices,
assessing their patients' conditions,
responding to their needs,
drawing alongside them as a friend and confidante,
helping them and their families come to terms
with what they are going through.
Give strength.
Give succour.

We think finally of fundraisers, volunteers,
charity shops and their managers,
charged with finding the money needed
to fund the hospice,
relying largely on public donations to pay the bills,
and finding it an increasing challenge in an era of
economic austerity.
Stir the hearts of all to respond generously,
so that the vital ministry hospices perform
may be able not only to continue,
but to expand,
offering help, hope and inner healing to as many as
possible in their time of need.
Give strength.
Give succour.
Amen.

48. Hospitals

(See also Ambulance staff and paramedics; Casualty departments; Health and healing; The National Health Service; Nurses)

Loving God,
hear our prayer for hospitals –
for those admitted to them as patients,
those who staff them,
those who run them
and those responsible for funding them.

We think of those receiving treatment:
those in Accident and Emergency;
those visiting as day patients for all kinds of procedures;
those waiting for or recovering from an operation;
those being treated for an acute or chronic disease;
those diagnosed with terminal illness.
In all they experience and the challenges they face,
support and help them.

We think of elderly patients,
many of them frail and vulnerable,
facing continuing decline,
often requiring ongoing care in a nursing
or residential home,
yet not finding anywhere able to take them in and look
after them.
In all they experience and the challenges they face,
support and help them.

We think of medical staff –
consultants, surgeons, clinicians, nurses and so many more –
striving to bring relief from pain,
improved health,

a better quality of life.
In all they experience and the challenges they face,
support and help them.

We think of counsellors, chaplains and clergy –
those who seek to minister to mind and spirit
rather than body,
bringing comfort, encouragement, strength and peace –
to be a listening ear,
a friend in adversity,
a compassionate and caring presence in what can
sometimes feel an impersonal environment.
In all they experience and the challenges they face,
support and help them.

We think of support staff –
cleaners, caterers, porters, cooks –
their work often overlooked,
taken for granted,
yet so vital and integral to patient health and safety
and to the smooth running of any hospital.
In all they experience and the challenges they face,
support and help them.

We think of Health Trust administrators and accountants,
those who must balance hospitals' books while responding
to increasing demand;
and we think of governments that must wrestle with the
pressing question of funding
in an era where most people live longer,
where money is short,
and where our lifestyles often contribute to health problems.
In all they experience and the challenges they face,
support and help them.
Amen.

49. The hungry

(*See also* Drought; The poor and needy; Social justice)

Lord of all,
hear our prayer for the hungry of our world.

We think of those whose harvest has failed,
destroyed by drought or engulfed by flood –
those who are left facing famine,
tormented each day by the gnawing ache of hunger,
forced to watch their malnourished children
fading before their eyes,
yearning for anything to fill their swollen bellies,
facing the prospect of starvation and death.
Bring change in our world,
and may the hungry be fed.

We think of those in countries devastated by war,
homes and livelihoods destroyed,
infrastructure shattered,
crops unsown or unharvested,
people once again left hungry and hopeless,
not knowing where the next meal is coming from,
dependent on aid supplies that too rarely get through.
Bring change in our world,
and may the hungry be fed.

We think of those who are too poor to feed themselves –
those whose labour is exploited,
those in countries lacking the resources or technology
to husband their land as they might,
those crippled by international debt,
those where regimes siphon off wealth
and leave citizens in need.
Bring change in our world,
and may the hungry be fed.

We think of those living rough on our streets,
eking out a living as beggars and vagrants,
hunger for them being an ever-present reality,
a square meal a luxury rather than expectation.
Bring change in our world,
and may the hungry be fed.

Reach out through government aid,
the work of charities,
the campaigns of pressure groups
and the generosity of ordinary people,
to bring an end to the misery of hunger –
to offer hope and help to all who are malnourished
and underfed.
Bring change in our world,
and may the hungry be fed.
Amen.

50. Hurting, those who are

(*See also* The bruised and broken)

Lord of all,
reach out to all in our world who are hurting.

To the sick and suffering,
bring hope,
bring help.

To the poor and hungry,
bring hope,
bring help.

To the weak and persecuted,
bring hope,
bring help.

To the fearful and worried,
bring hope,
bring help.

To the aged and infirm,
bring hope,
bring help.

To the oppressed and exploited,
bring hope,
bring help.

To the sorrowful and those who mourn,
bring hope,
bring help.

To the lonely and unloved,
bring hope,
bring help.

To the sick and suffering,
bring hope,
bring help.

To the homeless and refugees,
bring hope,
bring help.

To all in need,
all in despair,
all who are hurting,
bring hope,
bring help.
Amen.

51. An industrial dispute

(Enter the appropriate details in place of the ellipses below)

Lord of all,
hear our prayer today for those who seek to promote
harmony in industrial relations,
and especially those attempting to mediate in the current
dispute between ... and ...

Grant wisdom to arbitration services looking to bring
together the parties involved
and to broker an agreement;
the ability to deal honestly and fairly with both sides.
Help them truly to seek a just settlement
that is acceptable to all.
Though much divides,
may more unite.

Inspire a new spirit of openness among all involved
in the dispute:
a willingness to listen,
to consider,
to understand
and to compromise where necessary,
so that an escalation of industrial action
may be avoided if possible,
but unreasonable demands or ultimatums
be avoided equally.
Though much divides,
may more unite.

Give all involved the desire to enter into
constructive negotiations
rather than engage in divisive argument.
May they truly seek a lasting solution,
instead of resorting to brag and bluster,
political posturing or intransigence.
Though much divides,
may more unite.

Be with workers and families affected by strike action,
especially those whose jobs may hang in the balance,
whose livelihoods may be under threat,
and who may be facing very real hardship at this time.
Though much divides,
may more unite.

Give to management and employees a shared commitment
to the health of their company,
but also integrity in their dealings with each other.
Temper aspiration with realism,
the pursuit of profit with respect for workers' rights,
concern for the well-being of a few with a desire
for the good of all.
Though much divides,
may more unite.
Amen.

52. Injustice

(*See also* Social justice)

God of all,
we yearn for a fairer world,
a time when the injustice that scars so many human lives
will be put to an end.

We think of the countless millions on this planet
who are barely able to eke out a living –
who struggle each day,
with inadequate tools and insufficient resources,
to stave off the constant threat of hunger and disease.
In a world where many have too much
and more have too little,
grant that all may have enough.

We think of those whose harvest is bought up by
international companies and corporations,
purchased at low prices and then sold on for huge profits,
and we recognise that, too often,
we are the beneficiaries of a system that keeps the poor, poor
and the rich, rich.
In a world where many have too much
and more have too little,
grant that all may have enough.

We think of those denied hope and opportunity –
those who, through prejudice,
disability,
lack of education
or ill fortune,
struggle to fend for themselves,
and who find themselves beaten down by life,
with social and economic strictures preventing them
from getting back up again.
In a world where many have too much
and more have too little,
grant that all may have enough.

We think of those who strive to build a fairer world:
charities, campaigners, activists and governments –
all who seek to address issues of injustice and exploitation,
the wrongs that divide person from person and nation
from nation,
and that condemn many to a life of misery.
Help them to stir the consciences of all,
and through their efforts to bring about real
and lasting change.
In a world where many have too much
and more have too little,
grant that all may have enough.
Amen.

53. Interfaith dialogue

God of all,
we look to a time when religion will no longer divide
and alienate,
but instead will be a force for harmony and the good of all.

So, then, we bring before you religious leaders
and followers of the great faiths of this world.
Give them wisdom and humility,
the ability to recognise that,
however strong their convictions may be,
and however profound their insights,
they do not have a monopoly of truth,
but rather have something to learn from others
as well as something to teach them.
Speak *through* all.
Speak *to* all.

Teach us that, whatever our creed,
it is possible to disagree in love
and genuinely to respect the beliefs of others;
that though we may not share their opinions,
we can see where they are coming from
and be challenged by their practice and perceptions.
Speak *through* all.
Speak *to* all.

Challenge those who cling to intolerant
fundamentalist positions,
and all who use their faith as a prop to justify extremism.
Confront those who refuse to engage in dialogue;
those who automatically assume that they are right
and others are wrong,
and who see a questioning, enquiring faith
as a sign of weakness
rather than of strength.
Speak *through* all.
Speak *to* all.

Help believers everywhere to recognise that,
whatever their conception of God,
whatever their understanding of revelation,
whatever the extent of their faith,
it is always and necessarily incomplete,
for you are greater than the mind can fathom,
beyond our capacity ever to grasp fully,
and in understanding that,
may we learn better to understand each other.
Speak *through* all.
Speak *to* all.
Amen.

54. Justice and the judicial system

(See also Prisons)

Lord of all,
we pray for those involved in ensuring and upholding justice.

We think of the police,
tasked with administering the law,
tackling those who flout it,
investigating crimes
and apprehending criminals,
their work difficult and sometimes dangerous.
Give them wisdom and integrity,
that justice may be done.

We think of lawyers and solicitors,
entrusted with representing clients,
informing them of their rights,
advising on their case,
and ensuring they get a fair hearing
should they be taken to court.
Give them wisdom and integrity,
that justice may be done.

We think of judges, barristers and court officials –
all who must ensure that trials are conducted
impartially and smoothly,
who must advise jurors,
cross-examine witnesses,
or finally pronounce sentence.
Give them wisdom and integrity,
that justice may be done.

We pray for jurors,
assessing what they have heard,
weighing up the arguments,
sifting through the evidence
and finally delivering a verdict,
conscious that the future of the accused
depends on their decision.
Give them wisdom and integrity,
that justice may be done.

We think of prison and probation officers,
all who ensure that the penalty of the law
is paid and sentences served,
but who seek also to rehabilitate offenders,
to turn them away from crime
and to help them start a new life.
Give them wisdom and integrity,
that justice may be done.
Amen.

55. Leprosy sufferers

God of all,
hear our prayer today for those who suffer from leprosy in
all its many forms.

We think of those in our world who,
to our shame,
still live in fear of this debilitating disease,
so devastating in its impact,
yet relatively easy and cheap to treat,
and potentially to wipe out if there were sufficient
international resolve.
To all who continue to suffer,
give help and hope.

We think of those who continue to endure the stigma,
the nerve damage,
the sores,
the disfigurement,
the blindness,
associated with leprosy,
with all the attendant problems those bring.
To all who continue to suffer,
give help and hope.

We think of the various organisations across the world
committed to eradicating leprosy –
that work to bring help and healing to sufferers;
to heighten public awareness of the condition
and what can be done about it;
to raise funds for treatment and further research;
to help those whose lives have been blighted by the disease.
Guide them in all they do,
so that they may bring about real and lasting change.
To all who continue to suffer,
give help and hope.
Amen.

56. Lifeboat and air-sea rescue crews

God of all,
we think today of our coastal emergency services –
those who rescue people in peril, by sea or by air.

We think of lifeboat crews –
of the time they voluntarily give up to train
and respond to call-outs;
of the dangers they face
and rough weather they routinely brave;
of the courage and commitment they habitually display;
of the funds they need to raise to buy equipment
and to ensure it remains up to date.
In all they do,
guide and help them.

We think of air-sea rescue services –
of the skill of helicopter pilots,
manoeuvring in difficult and dangerous conditions;
of the bravery of crew who descend to stricken vessels
or casualties on clifftops
in order to winch people to safety.
In all they do,
guide and help them.

We think of the dedication to duty such work involves;
of the skill it calls for;
of the reassurance it gives to those who live
or work by the sea;
of the countless people who owe their lives to their
rescuers' courage and commitment.
In all they do,
guide and help them.

To all who serve in our coastal emergency services,
grant skill in their work,
provide them with the resources they need,
protect them from danger,
and reach out through them to help and save.
In all they do,
guide and help them.
Amen.

57. The lonely

God of love,
we remember today those who struggle with the burden
of loneliness.

We think of the elderly and housebound –
those who due to infirmity or ill health are unable to get
out as they used to,
to socialise with family and friends
or to be part of society in the way they once were,
sometimes spending days or even weeks without
meaningful human contact,
and often feeling themselves to be a burden
on those they *do* see.
Help them to cope with their isolation,
and to know themselves loved.

We think of those who have lost a loved one,
whose marriage or relationship with a partner
has broken down,
who are estranged by family feuds,
whose children have left home –
each yearning for the presence of those
they are separated from.
Help them to cope with their isolation,
and to know themselves loved.

We think of those who struggle to make friends,
who are too shy to build meaningful relationships,
who lack confidence in themselves,
who feel lonely even in a crowd.
Help them to cope with their isolation,
and to know themselves loved.

We think of those who live as refugees or migrants
in foreign lands,
who are treated with suspicion and hostility,
who feel their face does not fit and their presence
is not welcome.
Help them to cope with their isolation,
and to know themselves loved.

May those who are friendless find friendship,
those who are estranged find reconciliation,
those who doubt their worth find self-assurance,
those who mourn loved ones find comfort,
those who feel alone find companionship.
Help them to cope with their isolation,
and to know themselves loved.
Amen.

58. Marriage

Loving God,
we think today of marriage and all that it involves.

We bring before you those who are contemplating marriage
or settling down in a long-term relationship.
Give them genuine love,
real commitment,
an awareness of their strengths and weaknesses,
vices and virtues,
bad points as well as good,
that the relationship may be founded from the outset
on honesty,
understanding
and acceptance of the whole person, warts and all.
Nurture the gift of love,
and, whatever it has to face,
may it prove stronger than all.

We pray for those getting married.
May their wedding day be one of joy and celebration,
the start of a long and happy chapter in their lives –
a day to remember for themselves,
their family
and their friends.
Nurture the gift of love,
and, whatever it has to face,
may it prove stronger than all.

We pray for those experiencing marital difficulties –
those for whom the honeymoon period is over in every sense,
who have come up against the tensions as well as pleasures
of living together,
who find themselves at loggerheads,

forever arguing,
sulking,
even at times estranged,
such that they question the future of their relationship.
Nurture the gift of love,
and, whatever it has to face,
may it prove stronger than all.

We pray for those whose relationship
has broken down completely –
those mismatched in the first place;
those driven apart by financial pressures, family disputes,
illness or personal tragedy,
to the point that they seek time apart,
formal separation,
even divorce.
Nurture the gift of love,
and, whatever it has to face,
may it prove stronger than all.

We pray for those who prepare people
for marriage or life together –
those who conduct religious or civil ceremonies,
those who offer marriage guidance and counselling;
and we think also of those who represent clients
in divorce proceedings,
who negotiate settlements,
who guide people through the trauma of marital breakdown.
Help them to do their job wisely,
effectively
and compassionately.
Nurture the gift of love,
and, whatever it has to face,
may it prove stronger than all.
Amen.

59. Mental illness, those wrestling with

(*See also* Health and healing)

God of love,
we pray today for those who wrestle with mental illness.

We think of people suffering from clinical depression,
each day seeming as empty as the other,
devoid of hope or meaning,
life having lost all semblance of joy and fulfilment.
And we think, too, of their loved ones,
yearning to help,
longing to see them restored to the person they once were,
yet feeling helpless and hopeless,
unsure what to say or do,
wanting to offer support and encouragement
but afraid of making things worse rather than better.
Break into the night-time of despair, fear and confusion,
and bring a new dawn once more.

We think of those with common mental health disorders –
conditions like OCD, post-traumatic stress,
phobias and panic attacks,
each liveable with,
often hidden away from others,
yet destroying happiness and peace of mind,
eating away at the sufferer's quality of life,
sapping confidence and undermining self-esteem.
Break into the night-time of despair, fear and confusion,
and bring a new dawn once more.

We pray for those with eating disorders –
anorexia, bulimia, binge-eating disorder and the like –
those who feel driven by peer or media pressure,
bullying or abuse,

negative self-image,
stress or relationship problems,
to feast or fast,
to indulge or starve their body,
sinking into a spiral of destructive eating habits
and inexorable physical decline,
unless they are able to halt the cycle.
Break into the night-time of despair, fear and confusion,
and bring a new dawn once more.

We think of those suffering from severe mental health
problems –
psychosis, schizophrenia, bipolar disorder, mania –
especially those who will need to take medication
throughout their lives
and who may potentially be a danger to themselves
or to others.
Through counselling, drug therapy and practical support,
may they, wherever possible, be enabled to participate fully
in society,
their symptoms controlled,
their true self set free.
Break into the night-time of despair, fear and confusion,
and bring a new dawn once more.

Hear our prayer for all whose lives have been affected
by mental illness.
Help them and their families to come to terms
with their condition
and to respond to it positively,
so that they may find relief,
help
and hope.
Break into the night-time of despair, fear and confusion,
and bring a new dawn once more.
Amen.

60. The Middle East

Lord of all,
hear our prayer for the Middle East,
still racked today by so much tension and hatred.

We pray for the peoples of Palestine, Israel, Lebanon,
Syria, Iran and Iraq,
and of other nations surrounding these,
each coexisting uneasily together.
Bring harmony.
Bring lasting peace.

We pray for victims in the region of intolerance,
of violence,
of oppression,
of persecution.
Bring harmony.
Bring lasting peace.

We pray for an end to religious and political extremism,
to civil war and feuding,
to fear and suspicion,
to resorting to the bullet and bomb rather than
constructive dialogue.
Bring harmony.
Bring lasting peace.

We pray for politicians and leaders in the area,
and for those in the wider world with influence upon it.
Help them to see beyond narrow religious and
factional interest,
beyond long-held prejudice and traditional stereotypes,
and truly to seek a path towards respect,
reconciliation
and justice for all.
Bring harmony.
Bring lasting peace.
Amen.

61. Migrants

(See also Refugees)

Lord God,
we think today of all who have felt driven
to become migrants,
leaving behind their homes and homeland
in pursuit of a better life.

We think especially of those fleeing from war and terror:
those whose communities have been shattered by violence,
whose loved ones have been killed,
or who live each day in fear for their own life.
Give hope.
Bring new beginnings.

We think of those who risk their lives,
such is their desperation,
putting themselves in the hands of people smugglers,
venturing across the sea in ramshackle vessels
crammed to overflowing,
thousands lost to the waves.
And we think of others who have met with closed borders,
with rejection, abuse and hatred,
their plight insufficient to win hearts and minds,
or their numbers too many to cope with.
Give hope.
Bring new beginnings.

We think of immigrants in our own country –
those who have come to these shores seeking refuge
or simply a better standard of living
for themselves or their loved ones,
and ready often to accept hours and conditions of work
that few of us would contemplate:

part of an unseen economy we prefer to ignore
yet have come to depend on.
Give hope.
Bring new beginnings.

We think of the way migrants are so often viewed
with suspicion,
prejudice,
even malice,
some finding themselves the victims of jibes and insults,
others of threats and violence.
We pause for a moment to consider what it must feel like
to be in a different country,
with a different culture
and a different language from one's own,
in which one's very presence is resented by many.

Pause for silent reflection

Give hope.
Bring new beginnings.

Open our hearts to the stranger and the needy,
and help us to treat others as we would hope to be treated
in their place.
Give wisdom to all who must wrestle with the complex
question of migration
and the many issues associated with it,
but grant that their decisions,
and our attitudes,
will be shaped not by bigotry or narrow jingoism,
but by compassion, tolerance and a genuine concern for all.
Give hope.
Bring new beginnings.
Amen.

62. Natural disaster, those overwhelmed by

(*See also* Drought; Floods, those overwhelmed by)

(*Adapt the wording as appropriate, depending on the nature of the disaster – flood, fire, earthquake, tsunami, hurricane, tornado – and whether lives have been lost.*)

God of all,
we bring before you again the needs of the world,
and especially we think of those
[*insert name of country or place*]
whose lives have been overwhelmed by the disaster
of this past week.

We pray for those whose homes have been damaged
or destroyed,
whose livelihoods are gone,
who have witnessed so much that they worked for
and valued wrecked beyond repair,
who have seen friends or loved ones injured or killed,
who have been left shocked and bewildered by everything
they have seen and experienced.
Reach out to hold.
Reach out to help.

We pray for communities facing the massive task
of rebuilding and repair,
of restoring homes and infrastructure,
and we ask your guidance for all whose task it will be to
help in this –
government and politicians,
local authorities,
emergency services,

construction workers,
aid agencies.
Reach out to hold.
Reach out to help.

We pray for those with the equally challenging task of
ministering to the sick and injured,
of helping to mend broken bones and bodies,
to put back together broken lives,
to rekindle broken morale –
nurses,
doctors,
surgeons,
counsellors
and many more,
each seeking to bring help and relief.
Reach out to hold.
Reach out to help.

Be with all overwhelmed by this disaster
as they try to restore some semblance of normality
to their lives,
to adjust to their changed circumstances
and to rebuild for the future.
Give them comfort and reassurance,
strength and support,
love and guidance,
so that they may be able to do everything that can be done.
Reach out to hold.
Reach out to help.
Amen.

63. The news media

Loving God,
we pray today for the news media,
that it may discharge its responsibilities wisely.

We think of news and current affairs programmes on
television and radio,
dedicated to keeping us informed of world and home events,
of developments in important issues,
whether social, environmental, political or international.
Help them to do so in an informed
and thoughtful manner,
and as objectively as possible,
not moulded by government or party pressure,
by lobbyists, corporate interests or media moguls,
but seeking to present details to listeners and viewers
in such a way that they can assess these for themselves.
Whatever the media's goals,
may truth be first among them.

We think of newspapers and magazines,
too often influenced by political prejudice
or resorting to sensationalist headlines to boost sales –
misreporting and misrepresenting the facts,
stereotyping individuals and communities,
scaremongering and deceiving,
anything at times to prevent the truth from getting in the
way of a good story.
Help them to use their influence more prudently:
to offer more balanced and honest reporting,
to the ultimate good of all.
Whatever the media's goals,
may truth be first among them.

We think of journalists and editors competing against
each other for the best scoop,
the most eye-catching headline,
the most up-to-date news,
jostling perhaps for promotion
or fearful of others taking their job,
and so feeling under constant pressure to deliver,
even if that involves compromising their integrity.
Help them to set themselves standards,
and to stick to these though they may be tempted
to do otherwise.
Whatever the media's goals,
may truth be first among them.
Amen.

64. The National Health Service

(*See also* Ambulance staff and paramedics; GPs; Health and Healing; Hospitals)

Loving God,
hear our prayer for the National Health Service,
in all the pressures it is up against.

We think of consultants, surgeons, doctors and nurses
in our hospitals,
struggling to cope with growing demand
without commensurate funding;
of GP practices and their staff attempting to cope
with ever more patients;
of hospital departments endeavouring
to limit patient waiting times;
of officials responsible for approving
or rejecting new drugs and treatments,
needing to weigh up the costs and benefits
within a limited budget.
Through all they do,
bring help and healing.

We think of care workers in the community
seeking to support the old,
the disabled,
the chronically ill
or the dying,
striving to offer the best possible care within the constraints
of time and money.
Through all they do,
bring help and healing.

We think of ambulance drivers and paramedics,
dentists and physiotherapists,
psychiatrists and mental health workers –
all who minister to body, mind or soul.
Through all they do,
bring help and healing.

We think of NHS Trusts and their managers;
of administrators and support staff;
of those in charge of managing budgets,
allocating resources,
negotiating the prices of drugs and equipment,
employing personnel
and paying wages.
Through all they do,
bring help and healing.

Protect our Health Service,
so often taken for granted
but so vital,
and so valued when needed.
Give to decision-makers the vision, wisdom and courage
they need to safeguard its future,
and to ensure that it remains fit to respond
to the challenges of our time,
providing free quality care to all at the point of need.
Through all they do,
bring help and healing.
Amen.

65. Nurses

(*See also* Health and healing; Hospitals; The National
Health Service)

Lord of all,
hear our prayer today for those who serve as nurses.

We think of the different situations in which they work –
those on children's wards,
cancer wards,
surgical wards;
those in outpatients' clinics and facilities;
those caring in the community;
those who offer help and support to the elderly or infirm;
those in hospices or psychiatric hospitals;
those who provide care at home.
Through all who nurse the sick,
bring help and healing.

We think of the pressures nurses face –
the long hours,
the constant demands,
the unappealing tasks,
the emotional stresses,
the challenge of staff shortages,
the task of dealing with difficult patients.
Through all who nurse the sick,
bring help and healing.

We think of the ministry nurses perform –
reassuring the frightened,
comforting the sorrowful and bereaved,
easing pain,
administering treatment,
checking on patient safety and well-being –
a host of tasks so often taken for granted.
Through all who nurse the sick,
bring help and healing.

Encourage nurses in their work.
Equip them for the many duties entrusted to them.
Strengthen them to deal with the demands they face.
And enable them to bring relief,
in body, mind and spirit,
to those in their care.
Through all who nurse the sick,
bring help and healing.
Amen.

66. Nursing/residential care homes

(*See also* Dementia; The elderly)

God of all,
we pray today for those living or working in nursing
and care homes.

We think of those who are too infirm
to look after themselves;
of those with dementia,
needing constant care and attention;
of those who are unwell, requiring ongoing treatment;
of those who are temporary residents in such homes,
spending time there to give carers and family
a period of respite.
Whatever their situation,
**may residents always be treated with compassion
and respect.**

We think of those struggling to come to terms
with their new surroundings;
those who feel abandoned and unloved;
who feel shaken and confused;
who feel they have lost their independence,
their identity,
their dignity.
Whatever their situation,
**may residents always be treated with compassion
and respect.**

We pray for managers of these homes,
for care workers and nursing staff,
and for all who play a part behind the scenes,
cleaning,
cooking,
maintaining the premises,
and performing a host of other tasks
integral to residents' needs.
Whatever their situation,
**may residents always be treated with compassion
and respect.**

We think of the pressures faced by nursing
and care homes today:
the growing problem of funding and shortfalls
faced by local councils,
the challenge of recruiting caring and committed staff,
the increasing life expectancy of the population
and the growing demands and needs of elderly people.
Whatever their situation,
**may residents always be treated with compassion
and respect.
Amen.**

67. Paralysis

Lord of all,
we pray today for those who wrestle with paralysis.

We think of those who are born paralysed –
those having to cope from childhood with life in a
wheelchair,
with being dependent on others for many of the things
we take for granted.
Give help.
Give hope.

We think of those who are partially paralysed,
unable to walk but able to still use their hands and arms,
and we think of those totally paralysed,
trapped in a body that is unable to move.
Give help.
Give hope.

We think of those paralysed as the result of an accident,
a stroke,
multiple sclerosis,
cerebral palsy,
spina bifida,
motor neurone disease
or other illnesses.
Give help.
Give hope.

We think of those facing the prospect of paralysis,
able still to move but knowing that,
unless there are breakthroughs in treatment,
their mobility will gradually decrease
until it is gone altogether.
Give help.
Give hope.

We think of scientists and researchers:
those seeking new and more effective treatments;
those conducting pioneering research
into helping people walk again,
into reconnecting nerves,
implanting cells and restoring sensation,
into harnessing technology to reverse paralysis
and transform the lives of those facing it for ever.
Give help.
Give hope.
Amen.

68. Parents

(See also Children leaving home)

Loving God,
hear our prayer today for parents.

We think of new parents –
excited,
yet daunted by a new addition to their family,
by the challenge of sleepless nights,
by the demands a young baby will inevitably make,
by the responsibilities, alongside the privilege,
of parenthood.
To parents everywhere,
give wisdom,
give guidance,
give love.

We think of parents bringing up their children,
seeking to give them the best start in life,
to prepare them for school and beyond,
to provide for their needs, physical and emotional,
to give them the security of a happy and settled home life,
and to be a loving focus on which they can depend.
To parents everywhere,
give wisdom,
give guidance,
give love.

We think of parents whose children are leaving home –
those coming to terms with the end of an era;
with the fragmenting of the family life
they have come to know and love;
with no longer sharing with their children as they once did;
with living far away and not seeing each other for long
spells at a time.
To parents everywhere,
give wisdom,
give guidance,
give love.

We think of parents who have grown old,
who have become ill or infirm,
who are now dependent on their children,
who feel themselves to be a burden.
To parents everywhere,
give wisdom,
give guidance,
give love.

We pray for parents in broken relationships –
fathers or mothers denied access to their children
or only able to see them for a short time each week;
those who have become estranged as a result of breakups;
those who witness their children becoming confused,
hurt or disturbed
as they are caught up in the bitterness of separation
or divorce.
To parents everywhere,
give wisdom,
give guidance,
give love.
Amen.

69. Peacemakers

(*See also* The armed forces; An industrial dispute; The
Middle East; War, people and places broken by; War and
peace; World peace)

Lord of all,
we pray today for those who seek to live as peacemakers.

We think of those who try to make peace in daily life –
to calm tempers,
defuse an argument,
bring together those who have grown estranged,
conciliate in disputes between families, friends
and neighbours.
Give them sensitivity in each situation,
understanding of opposing points of view,
and wisdom concerning how to respond.
Through their efforts,
bring peace.

We think of those who attempt to arbitrate in industrial
or work-related disputes –
between employer and employee,
management and trade union,
one worker and another.
Give them tact and diplomacy;
a willingness to compromise where appropriate,
but equally the ability to be firm and decisive
when necessary;
a genuine desire to find a solution acceptable to all
but equally a determination to be fair.
Through their efforts,
bring peace.

We think of those who strive to further world peace –
government leaders at summits and conferences;
envoys and diplomats seeking to defuse tensions
or end conflict;
peace-keeping forces sent into dangerous situations
to establish or maintain a truce;
delegates discussing arms treaties
and a reduction of weapons;
anti-war protestors and disarmament campaigners –
all who, in different ways, endeavour to heal the wounds
that divide us.
Through their efforts,
bring peace.

To all who work to promote unity,
to reconcile individuals, factions, creeds or countries,
give guidance, help and inspiration.
Grant humility in approaching others,
integrity in dealing with them
and sensitivity in seeking solutions –
the right words to say and deeds to match them –
so that discord may be overcome
and harmony be established between all.
Through their efforts,
bring peace.
Amen.

70. The persecuted

(*See also* The exploited and abused; Homophobia;
Migrants; Refugees)

Lord God,
we think today of all whose lives are overshadowed
by persecution.

We think of those living in places racked by civil war,
all too many innocent people caught up in the violence,
hatred and bloodshed,
unable to venture out safely on the street
but feeling equally unsafe in their own homes.
Give strength in adversity
and hope for the future.

We think of those who live as oppressed minorities,
viewed with suspicion on account of their creed, colour,
caste or culture;
subject to abuse and hostility;
denied meaningful employment or opportunity;
fearful of what each day might bring to them.
Give strength in adversity
and hope for the future.

We think of those who are persecuted
on account of their convictions,
their beliefs,
their faith –
denied freedom of worship and expression.
Give strength in adversity
and hope for the future.

We think of those who are bullied –
at school,
in their workplace,
in their relationships –
victims of cruelty, prejudice or insensitivity.
Give strength in adversity
and hope for the future.

Give help to all who are persecuted –
the courage, comfort and support they need
to get through,
and the prospect of an end to their trials
and of a better tomorrow.
Give strength in adversity
and hope for the future.
Amen.

71. The physically disabled

Lord God,
hear our prayer for the disabled.

We think of those born with a disability –
those who have had to cope with it
since their earliest years,
never experiencing the full health
that most of us take for granted.
Help them, whatever their condition,
to live life as fully as possible.
Give help.
Give strength.

We think of those disabled through illness or injury –
losing a limb in an accident,
paralysed by a fall or disease,
maimed in military service,
incapacitated by a stroke.
Help them to deal with the psychological and physical
impact of their disability,
and, however broken they may be, still to feel whole.
Give help.
Give strength.

We think of those who work to help the disabled,
developing prosthetic limbs,
designing wheelchairs,
offering physiotherapy,
researching new treatments,
promoting opportunities for sport,
providing disabled access.
Work through them to bring increased mobility,
renewed motivation,
an enhanced quality of life
and encouragement for the future.
Give help.
Give strength.
Amen.

72. The police

Loving God,
we pray today for those who serve in the police force.

We think of the routine work they do:
controlling traffic,
patrolling areas,
stewarding events,
maintaining a presence on the streets.
In all their work,
be with them.

We think of their work in fighting crime:
of those in ongoing investigations,
making house-to-house enquiries,
conducting a search,
taking statements,
following up leads,
arresting suspects.
Give them wisdom, integrity and dedication.
In all their work,
be with them.

We think of those working in upsetting
and traumatic circumstances:
attending a road accident,
uncovering the scene of a violent crime,
conducting a missing child enquiry,
breaking news to a family of the death of a loved one.
Give them strength and support,
and help them to deal with such moments
sensitively at all times.
In all their work,
be with them.

We think of those working in potentially dangerous situations:
apprehending a violent offender,
dealing with riots and social unrest,
working undercover,
infiltrating terrorist cells.
Watch over them and grant them protection.
In all their work,
be with them.

Give all police the ability to be even-handed
in everything they do,
the courage to do their work thoroughly,
the insight to do it wisely
and the resolve to do it fairly.
In all their work,
be with them.
Amen.

73. The poor and needy

(See also The Deprived; Injustice; Poorly paid workers;
Social justice)

Lord of all,
we bring before you those who live in poverty;
those for whom the comforts of this world
are a distant dream.

We think of the poor in our own country –
those who sleep rough at night or in shelters,
migrant workers paid less than a living wage,
parents struggling to make ends meet,
families living on or below the poverty line.
Grant them help.
Grant them hope.

We think of those in the wider world,
so many wrestling with unimaginable hardship,
surviving on means and in conditions that we can
scarcely countenance.
People up against famine, disease,
injustice and exploitation,
livelihoods ravaged by war,
crops decimated by natural disaster,
tools for cultivation inadequate for the job in hand,
economics stacked against them.
Grant them help.
Grant them hope.

We think of those who strive to bring change –
who campaign for justice,
raise funds to provide relief,
work for charities and aid agencies,
encourage Fair Trade,
share skills and resources,
offer shelter and support,
work for peace and reconciliation,
or challenge economic systems
and pioneer new models of trade.
Grant them help.
Grant them hope.

Grant that the day will come when this world's bounty
will be shared more fairly:
when no one needs to live in poverty,
when opportunity is truly open to all
and no one is condemned to starvation, disease,
need or despair.
Reach out, then, to all who are poor,
and help us to do the same.
Grant them help.
Grant them hope.
Amen.

74. Poorly paid workers

(See also Injustice; Social justice; The underpaid)

Lord of all,
hear our prayer for all who are poorly paid.

We think of those getting by on the minimum wage,
those living in poverty,
those holding down two or three jobs involving long
and unsocial hours,
those on zero-hour contracts offering flexibility
but little security to them or their families.
Give help.
Give hope.

We think of those who lack the education,
qualifications or nous for most jobs,
condemned instead to dead-end work,
often mind-numbingly repetitive,
and once again at the bottom of the pay scale,
with little if any opportunity to work one's way up.
Give help.
Give hope.

We pray for those in other countries working in
overcrowded factories or sweatshops,
and for those exploited by large companies and
corporations,
denied a fair price for their produce,
living still in penury while profits go elsewhere.
Give help.
Give hope.

Though there will always be rich and poor,
the privileged and the underprivileged,
may there also be a desire for greater justice,
the resolve to help those least able to help themselves,
so that none is left to go to the wall
and all are fairly rewarded for their labour.
Give help.
Give hope.
Amen.

75. Pornography

(*See also* The exploited and abused)

Loving God,
we pray today for all those affected by the industry of
pornography.

We think of young men and women exploited for sex
from other countries,
lured from their homeland by the promise of a new life
only to find themselves forced to parade their body,
to take part in acts of degradation,
to abandon their principles and scruples,
in order to survive.
Reach out to help.
Reach out to save.

We pray for those who are addicted to pornography –
who download it on their computers,
who view it at every opportunity,
who have come to see voyeurism as the norm
rather than as an aberration.
Reach out to help.
Reach out to save.

We pray for those corrupted by pornography,
their appetites twisted and perverted,
their sexual relationships shaped by images they've seen,
their partners viewed simply as sex objects.
Reach out to help.
Reach out to save.

We think of those troubled about pornography –
parents worried about what their children might
be viewing,
young people feeling pushed by peer pressure into sharing
explicit images of themselves,
individuals who know they have a problem
but who are struggling to overcome it.
Reach out to help.
Reach out to save.

We think of those who offer guidance and counselling
to those affected by pornography;
of those who fight against sexual exploitation;
of those who attempt to police the internet;
and of those who fight against child pornography
in particular.
Reach out to help.
Reach out to save.
Amen.

76. Pregnancy and infertility

Lord God,
we think today of those who are pregnant,
and of those who long to have children but struggle to do so,
or try to conceive in vain.

We think of those expecting their first child,
full of hope and excitement,
wrestling perhaps with a few nerves –
the pain of childbirth,
the way their lives will be changed for ever,
the extra responsibilities that a baby will bring –
but filled nonetheless with anticipation.
In all they go through,
be with them.

We think of mothers giving birth –
the discomfort,
effort,
pain –
but then the joy,
relief
and unsurpassable sense of wonder.
In all they go through,
be with them.

We think of those taking a new baby home for the first time –
the feeding,
the changing of nappies,
the long sleepless nights;
but also the countless delights,
the developing of that unique bond between parent and child,
the pride and contentment.
In all they go through,
be with them.

We think of those who suffer the trauma of a stillborn child,
their dreams shattered,
their joy replaced by shock, grief and disbelief;
everything they had hoped for taken away,
life suddenly seeming bleak and empty.
In all they go through,
be with them.

We pray for those being given fertility treatment,
hoping against hope that it will be successful,
attempting to maximise the possibility of it working,
waiting each month for the results of tests
or for signs of hope.
In all they go through,
be with them.

We pray for those denied the joy of motherhood –
coming to terms with their infertility,
often spending huge sums in the hope of realising
their dreams
only for all treatment to prove hopeless.
Help them to come to terms with their sense of loss,
with the knowledge that so many of their dreams
will never come to fruition.
In all they go through,
be with them.
Amen.

77. Prisons

(*See also* Justice and the judicial system)

Lord of all,
we think today of prisons:
of their importance in society,
but equally of the testing challenges they present.

We think of prison officers and staff,
and of the difficult and demanding job they do each day –
their need to stay vigilant at all times,
alert to smuggled drugs and weapons,
the threat of violence against themselves or other prisoners,
their need to balance idealism and realism.
May justice be done,
but new beginnings also be made possible.

We think of prisoners:
some hardened to a life of crime;
some violent and dangerous;
some so used to prison life they know little else;
some first-time offenders, ashamed and scared
of what they may face inside;
others ending their sentences
and looking to begin a new life,
but facing prejudice and suspicion,
problems in finding employment and acceptance in society.
May justice be done,
but new beginnings also be made possible.

We think of governments and politicians,
responsible for tackling crime
and for addressing issues of prison overcrowding,
staffing and funding;
with ensuring safe and secure incarceration of prisoners
that the due penalty of the law may be paid,
but also with rehabilitating offenders into the community.
May justice be done,
but new beginnings also be made possible.
Amen.

78. Racism

(See also Barriers in society, those working to break down)

God of all,
hear our prayer for all who suffer as victims of racism.

We think of places where racial differences remain
stark and divisive,
where people are daily victimised and persecuted on
account of their skin,
where they walk in fear for their lives,
where there have been attempts at systematic genocide.
Wherever such division remains,
may your love unite.

We pray for those who face racial prejudice and
discrimination –
those who are denied their human rights,
who are treated as second-class citizens,
who are harassed, abused, ill-treated.
Wherever such division remains,
may your love unite.

We pray for victims of anti-Semitism,
so long a blight on our world
and remaining all too real today,
lessons of the past still not learnt.
And we pray also for the Middle East,
racked by so much hatred, suspicion,
intolerance and injustice.
Wherever such division remains,
may your love unite.

We think of victims of racism in our own country –
against Asian communities, exacerbated by fears of
religious extremism,
against black people, perpetuated by negative stereotypes,
against migrants, fuelled by political scaremongering.
Wherever such division remains,
may your love unite.

Help us to see the racism that lurks within ourselves,
typically unacknowledged,
pushed to one side,
often unrecognised,
sometimes denied,
but subtly influencing our attitudes
and potentially alienating us from others.
Wherever such division remains,
may your love unite.

Help all to see beyond the colour of people's skin,
the nature of their dress,
the tenets of their religion,
the characteristics of their culture,
and to see the person underneath,
beyond race or culture.
Wherever such division remains,
may your love unite.
Amen.

79. Refugees

(*See also* The homeless; Migrants; The poor and needy;
Social justice)

Lord God,
we pray today for all who live as refugees.

For those forced to abandon their homes
due to war and violence,
hear our prayer.

For those driven from their country by famine,
hear our prayer.

For those fleeing persecution,
hear our prayer.

For those in refugee camps, rife with disease,
hear our prayer.

For those who do not know where the next meal
is coming from,
hear our prayer.

For those whose loved ones are dying of sickness
or starvation,
hear our prayer.

For those turned away where they have sought refuge,
hear our prayer.

For those transported from their countries in airless lorries
or unseaworthy vessels,
hear our prayer.

For those with nowhere to call their home,
hear our prayer.

For those far from family and friends,
hear our prayer.

For those who have left homeland and livelihood,
hear our prayer.

For those who see no prospect of returning to their old life,
hear our prayer.

For those increasingly treated with suspicion and hostility,
hear our prayer.

For those seeking to make a fresh start
after all they have faced,
hear our prayer.
Amen.

80. Scientists and researchers

Lord God,
hear our prayer today for those involved in the field of
scientific research.

We think of the advances that have been made over the years –
the discoveries achieved,
the mysteries unlocked,
the possibilities opened up –
and we ask you to give vision, wisdom and sensitivity
to all scientists,
that they may be equipped to dig deeper
and explore further
so as to help us understand better the wonders
of our universe,
and the ways we can harness and shape them for the
common good.
Give to all an enquiring mind
and a discerning spirit.

We think of the benefits science has brought to humanity –
the medical breakthroughs
that have eradicated many diseases
and made countless others treatable;
the technologies that have transformed standards of living;
the gadgets and labour-saving devices we take for granted;
the inventions that have made possible the world as we
know it today.
Guide those who continue to study, experiment and
research into new ideas,
that they may find innovative solutions
to problems that still confront us
and equip us better to respond to the challenges
of our modern age.
Give to all an enquiring mind
and a discerning spirit.

We think of the moral and ethical conundrums
raised by science:
developments that raise concerns as well as opportunities,
dilemmas as well as advances,
troubling questions as well as liberating answers.
Give humility to scientists as they wrestle with these,
a proper sense of responsibility
and the ability to make wise decisions.
Give to all an enquiring mind
and a discerning spirit.
Amen.

81. Sexism

(See also Barriers in society, those working to break down)

Lord of all,
hear our prayer today for victims of sexism,
and for all who work to break down gender prejudice
and discrimination
wherever it still exists in our society.
To women everywhere
grant the respect they are due.

We think of the ways women have been discriminated
against in so many walks of life,
their talents underrated,
their gifts overlooked,
their creativity muzzled,
their potential ignored.
To women everywhere
grant the respect they are due.

We think of women still expected to conform
to gender stereotypes;
of those doing the same work as men
yet being paid significantly less for it;
of those who have reached a glass ceiling,
not being considered for top jobs;
of those denied opportunities because they are women.
To women everywhere
grant the respect they are due.

We think of those who feel themselves to be treated
as sex objects,
not taken seriously on account of their gender;
of those who feel demeaned by sexist comments
and attitudes;
of those who feel vulnerable to the male gaze.
To women everywhere
grant the respect they are due.

Open the eyes of all to the injustices women have faced
across the centuries,
and to the prejudices that continue to lurk
unchallenged to this day.
And grant guidance and help to those who strive
to right such wrongs,
so that there may truly be equality of opportunity,
equality of respect,
equality of rewards.
To women everywhere
grant the respect they are due.
Amen.

82. The sick and suffering

(*See also* Health and healing; Hospitals; Trouble, those facing times of (1) and (2))

Lord of all,
we remember today those who are sick.

We think of those suffering from minor illnesses,
not serious or life threatening,
but nonetheless unpleasant,
dragging the sufferer down
and undermining their health and happiness.
We remember especially in a moment of quietness those
known to us.

Pause for silent reflection

Bring help.
Bring healing.

We think of those with more serious conditions –
waiting perhaps for a diagnosis or operation,
wrestling with acute or chronic conditions,
coming to terms with cancer or the onset of dementia,
facing the prospect of aggressive and debilitating treatment
or a long and gradual decline.
Again, we pause to remember those known to us.

Pause for silent reflection

Bring help.
Bring healing.

We think of those who are terminally ill,
confronted by the stark reality of death,
fearful of what they might have to endure
and grieving at the prospect of leaving loved ones behind –
desperately hoping against hope that some new treatment
might be found.
We pause again to remember those we know in special
need at this time.

Pause for silent reflection

Bring help.
Bring healing.

We think of those who minister to the sick:
GPs and health professionals,
doctors and nurses,
surgeons and consultants,
together with all who seek to minister to mind
as well as body,
offering emotional and practical support.
Through their work bring relief and comfort,
strength and succour,
health and wholeness.
Bring help.
Bring healing.
Amen.

83. Social justice

(See also Deprivation; The hungry; Injustice; The poor and needy; Poorly paid workers; The underpaid; World, seeking real and lasting change in)

God of all,
hear our prayer today for social justice.

In a world of haves and have nots,
of rich and poor,
of massive wealth and grinding poverty,
bring justice,
a fair deal for all.

In a world where the labour of many is exploited,
where workers receive a pittance
while multinational companies and corporations
rake in vast profits,
bring justice,
a fair deal for all.

In a world of prejudice and discrimination,
where people are denied opportunity,
or are ridiculed and persecuted,
due to their race, gender, sexuality, creed or culture,
bring justice,
a fair deal for all.

In a world of oppression,
where people are still in some places ruled by dictators,
denied their human rights,
subject to draconian laws,
kept in subjugation,
bring justice,
a fair deal for all.

In a world of disease,
where thousands die for lack of proper sanitation,

proper diet,
proper medicine,
proper healthcare,
bring justice,
a fair deal for all.

In a world of hunger,
where countless people lack the resources they need
to feed themselves,
where parents strive in vain to provide the next meal,
where multitudes face starvation,
bring justice,
a fair deal for all.

In a world of inequality,
where some enjoy the best education,
the best opportunities,
the best lifestyle,
while others are disadvantaged from the start,
bring justice,
a fair deal for all.

In a world of greed, crime and corruption,
where people cheat,
steal,
lie,
dissemble,
to secure what they cannot gain by honest means,
bring justice,
a fair deal for all.

In a world of so much beauty but so much ugliness,
so much good but so much bad,
so much that is right but so much that is wrong,
bring justice,
a fair deal for all.
Amen.

84. Social workers

Lord of all,
hear our prayers for those who work in the difficult and
demanding sphere of social work.

We think of those who work with the elderly –
identifying those who need care and support
and ensuring they receive it;
seeking ways to improve their quality of life;
protecting them from danger;
assisting in practical issues;
offering counselling and support.
In all they do,
grant them wisdom, guidance and help.

We think of those working with young people –
assessing those at risk of abuse or neglect,
and stepping in when needed;
supporting foster-parents and those who seek to adopt;
helping those with disabilities, mental health issues
or other difficulties;
counselling and rehabilitating young offenders;
building relationships with those damaged
or traumatised by their life experiences.
In all they do,
grant them wisdom, guidance and help.

We think of those who deal with adults –
seeking to help refugees and asylum seekers;
those who feel socially excluded;
families at risk of breakdown;
carers in need of support;
those addicted to alcohol, drugs or other substances;
those with learning difficulties, a mental health problem
or a physical disability.
In all they do,
grant them wisdom, guidance and help.

Support and strengthen all social workers,
so that they may do their work wisely and well,
protecting where necessary,
encouraging where possible,
assisting where they are able
and making important decisions where they have to.
In all they do,
grant them wisdom, guidance and help.
Amen.

85. Surgeons

(See also Health and healing; Hospitals)

Lord of all,
we bring before you today those who work as surgeons.

We think of those in training,
those at medical college or completing their studies
as junior doctors,
watching and learning from others,
witnessing operations
or taking their first tentative steps towards
conducting one themselves.
Guide them in their learning,
focus their minds
and help them to acquire the skills they need
to do their job well.
In all they do,
equip and enable them.

We think of those conducting surgery –
of the complications they may come up against,
the conditions they will treat,
the concentration they must show,
the difference they will make to so many patients' lives.
Give them dedication, patience and wisdom.
In all they do,
equip and enable them.

We think of the pressures surgeons face –
the huge daily weight of responsibility,
the risks that are always present,
the hopes and fears of family and relatives,
the trauma of losing a patient on the table
and the horror of making a mistake.
Help them to cope with the burden they bear
and not to buckle under the strain.
In all they do,
equip and enable them.

Give to all surgeons a real sense of calling,
and keep their skills fresh across the years.
Inspire them through the healing and wholeness
they help to make possible –
relief from pain, injury and disease
transforming people's lives.
In all they do,
equip and enable them.
Amen.

86. Teachers

Lord God,
we bring before you today those entrusted with the task
of teaching.

We think of nursery and primary school teachers,
entrusted with helping to shape young lives in their
formative years,
of introducing them to the delights of language and stories,
of giving them simple but vital tools of knowledge
that will last for a lifetime.
Give them patience and inspiration
to nurture those in their care.
Speak *to* them.
Speak *through* them.

We think of junior school teachers,
tasked with carrying forward the next stage
of youthful development,
helping children to learn skills in maths and literacy,
and to gain their first real insights
into numerous other subjects.
Give them insight and sensitivity,
so that they will help not just knowledge to grow
but the young people in their classes, also.
Speak *to* them.
Speak *through* them.

We think of those in secondary schools
and sixth-form colleges,
preparing young people for the world of work
or further study,
seeking to stretch their minds,
broaden their horizons,
deepen their understanding
and enrich their awareness.
Give them the wisdom and dedication they need
to do their job well.
Speak *to* them.
Speak *through* them.

We think of those in our colleges and universities –
those who seek to hone skills for working life,
and those who strive to take learning further,
refining knowledge and understanding.
Give them the ability to communicate,
enthuse and encourage,
so that their students may fulfil their true potential.
Speak *to* them.
Speak *through* them.

Grant your help to all who seek to pass on knowledge,
to share what they have learnt with others.
Equip them to meet the challenges they will face,
and help them to honour the privilege
yet responsibility of teaching.
Speak *to* them.
Speak *through* them.
Amen.

87. Terrorism

(See also Extremism)

Lord of all,
we bring before you today victims of terrorism,
those whose lives have been turned upside down in the
name of religion or politics.

We think of those who have been killed –
husbands, wives, parents, children:
people of different faiths,
different races,
different cultures.
Overcome the forces of hatred,
and heal our broken world.

We think of those who have lost loved ones,
those who have been left disabled or maimed,
those traumatised by what they have seen or heard,
those who have had to step into the carnage
and bring relief.
Overcome the forces of hatred,
and heal our broken world.

We think of the callous acts that have scarred our world
in recent years:
of buildings destroyed,
of planes, trains and buses blown up,
of people hacked to death or gunned down in the street,
of countless victims of bullet and bomb.
Overcome the forces of hatred,
and heal our broken world.

We think of those in the security services,
charged with seeking to ensure such atrocities
do not occur again,
their work difficult, demanding and dangerous,
calling for sacrifices that few of us will ever
begin to understand,
let alone experience.
Give them wisdom, guidance, protection and support.
Overcome the forces of hatred,
and heal our broken world.

We think of governments and world leaders,
those faced with the complex affairs
of international relations.
Help them to make wise decisions based not simply on
national or political interest,
nor solely on economic advantage,
but on a desire to build a world in which the seeds of
terrorism will struggle to put down root.
Overcome the forces of hatred,
and heal our broken world.

We think finally of terrorists themselves,
those who believe that one wrong can put right another,
that the murder of innocents can ever be justified,
that atrocities can be seen as serving God
and suicide attacks offer a pathway to heaven.
Teach them that their actions are a denial of their faith
and an affront to you,
and that to lose sight of this is to lose sight of all.
Overcome the forces of hatred,
and heal our broken world.
Amen.

88.   Trouble, those facing times of (1)

Loving God,
we pray today for all those facing times of difficulty
in their life.

We think of those experiencing financial hardship,
those worried about losing their job,
those facing unemployment,
those who are in debt,
those on the verge of bankruptcy.
Reach out to hold.
Reach out to help.

We think of those experiencing relationship problems –
estrangement from their partner,
rebelliousness from children or intransigence from parents,
family feuds,
bullying at home, school or work,
betrayal by friends or colleagues,
or difficulty in building friendships
and coping with company.
Reach out to hold.
Reach out to help.

We think of those overcome by depression,
those wrestling with mental health problems,
those for whom life is a constant battle
against inner demons,
a dark tunnel from which they see no hope
of ever emerging.
Reach out to hold.
Reach out to help.

We pray for those who are unwell –
those struck down by serious disease,
those awaiting a diagnosis or operation,
those receiving treatment for cancer,
those with debilitating chronic conditions
and those with a terminal illness.
Reach out to hold.
Reach out to help.

We think of those troubled about loved ones,
worried about pressures they're facing,
concerned about them leaving home,
fearful for their health
or mourning those who have died.
Reach out to hold.
Reach out to help.

In a moment of silence, we think especially of those
known to us –
those for whom life is hard at the moment.

Pause for silent reflection

Reach out to hold.
Reach out to help.

To all facing times of trouble,
circumstances that concern and worry them,
that test them to the limit,
give strength, support and succour.
Reach out to hold.
Reach out to help.
Amen.

89. Trouble, those facing times of (2)

Loving God,
we pray for those facing times of trouble.

We think of those in places torn by hatred,
intolerance,
division,
violence;
those in lands ravaged by hunger,
oppression,
disease,
injustice;
those in countries broken by drought,
famine,
war,
exploitation.
To all for whom life is dark,
bring new light,
new life.

We think of those coping with difficulties
in their relationships;
those whose job is under threat
or who find themselves unemployed;
those nursing sick or incapacitated loved ones
or who are ill themselves;
those coming to terms with the death of a loved one
or with the prospect of their own death.
To all for whom life is dark,
bring new light,
new life.

We think of victims of crime,
abuse,
rape,
injustice;
of those who are haunted by memories of the past;
of those held captive by fears and worry;
of those struggling with mental illness;
of those who feel at the end of their tether
and unable to continue.
To all for whom life is dark,
bring new light,
new life.
Amen.

90. The underpaid

(see also Poorly paid workers)

Lord of all,
we bring to you the underpaid in society.

We think of those who work long and often
antisocial hours,
their work often dull and monotonous,
yet who take home barely the minimum wage,
each day a struggle to make ends meet,
their labour seeming to be taken for granted.
To all who work
give just reward for their labours.

We think of those working short-term
or zero-hour contracts,
many having to hold down two or even more jobs
to get by,
balancing one with another,
paid as little as employers can get away with,
often wearied to the point of exhaustion.
To all who work
give just reward for their labours.

We think of those in dead-end jobs with little hope of
raising themselves up;
those lacking the qualifications, confidence or opportunity
to do something else
and so condemned each day to perform the same routine,
the same drudgery,
for the lowest of wages.
To all who work
give just reward for their labours.

We think of the great and growing divide in our society
between rich and poor,
the haves and have nots:
those for whom a second home is almost an expectation,
and those glad to have anywhere to call home;
those for whom dining out in luxury is taken for granted,
and those who wonder where their next meal is
coming from;
those who look forward to a comfortable early retirement,
and those for whom old age will bring penury;
those who will never go short,
and those who will never have anywhere near enough.
Help us to build a fairer society,
a more just system in which none will have too much
and all will have sufficient;
in which a fair day's work will receive a fair day's pay,
and in which wealth will truly be shared by all.
To all who work
give just reward for their labours.
Amen.

91. The unemployed

Lord of all,
we think today of those who are unemployed,
with all the implications which that entails for themselves
and their families.

We think of those who live in regions where local industry
has collapsed:
miners, shipbuilders, steelworkers and the like –
their skills no longer valued or needed,
their traditional source of income and employment
plucked from them,
a whole culture, way of life, discontinued,
meaning the need to retrain and often move away
in search of work.
Give hope.
Give help.

We think of those who have struggled to learn new skills
or adjust to changing times,
having to spend months, even years, instead on benefits,
and wrestling as a result with a sense of embarrassment,
frustration
and despair
at being unable to provide for their family.
We think of all who long to work,
yet are denied the opportunity to do so.
Give hope.
Give help.

We think of those who have been laid off
or made redundant,
left reeling in a state of shock and uncertainty,
struggling to cope with the stigma of unemployment
and the lack of purpose and identity that it brings
in its wake –
their jobs the victims of cutbacks, mergers,
restructuring or companies going under.
We think especially of those who are older,
finding it harder than most to adapt,
and coming up against discrimination
on account of their age.
Give hope.
Give help.

We think of those who can no longer work
because of illness or disability,
their condition preventing them
from doing the job they once did,
forced instead to rely on state assistance
that is becoming ever tighter,
facing added anxiety and insecurity
on top of what they are already going through.
Give hope.
Give help.

For all who are unemployed,
and all who are affected by their plight –
families and friends, towns and communities –
grant provision in time of need,
and new opportunities:
the genuine prospect of change.
Give hope.
Give help.
Amen.

92. Veterinary surgeons

(*See also* Animal welfare)

Lord of all,
we pray today for veterinary surgeons.

We think of those who work with small animals at
practices across the country –
those entrusted by so many with the welfare of their pets;
with diagnosing what's wrong with them
when they are sick;
with prescribing treatment or operating on them
where necessary;
with carrying out health checks and vaccinations;
with putting seriously injured or terminally ill animals
to sleep.
In all they do,
give them skill, guidance and wisdom.

We think of those who work with farm animals,
those employed by zoos or racecourses,
those who must monitor stock for signs of disease or
mistreatment,
those responsible for ensuring public health and hygiene
laws are adhered to
and that animal welfare is paramount.
In all they do,
give them skill, guidance and wisdom.

We think of those who work at animal rescue centres,
taking in a variety of sick or injured creatures –
birds tarred by oil,
animals struck by vehicles,
pets neglected by their owners.
In all they do,
give them skill, guidance and wisdom.

We think, finally, of vets involved in teaching and research,
training new recruits to the profession,
investigating and trialling new forms of treatment,
seeking cures to currently intractable conditions.
In all they do,
give them skill, guidance and wisdom.
Amen.

93. The visually impaired

Loving God,
hear our prayer today for the visually impaired.

We think of the partially sighted –
those who can see something of the world around them
but not enough to enjoy it as fully or as easily as others;
those for whom their condition makes difficult tasks that
most of us take for granted.
Give help.
Give hope.

We thank of those with macular degeneration,
glaucoma,
cataracts
or other eye conditions:
those waiting for operations to restore the quality
of their vision,
or taking medication to help control it,
and those coming to terms with the prospect of gradually
declining sight,
with everything that entails.
Give help.
Give hope.

We think of those who cannot see at all –
those born without sight,
those who have lost it through illness or injury,
having to cope with life despite this disability,
with situations and problems that most of us would never
give a thought to.
Give help.
Give hope.

We think of opticians in their vital work of monitoring people's vision –
spotting problems and advising on treatment;
of eye surgeons and consultants,
helping to restore sight through operations
and other procedures;
of scientists and researchers,
seeking ways to reverse damage,
save sight,
and even give it to those who have never seen before.
Give help.
Give hope.
Amen.

94. War and peace

(*See also* The armed forces; Barriers in society, those
working to break down; Peacemakers; War, people and
places broken by; World peace)

Lord of all,
we think today of places still torn by war and hatred,
craving peace, yet still racked by violence.

We pray for those living close to arenas of combat –
those whose homes and communities have been destroyed,
who leave each day amid scenes of continuing division,
mistrust,
fear,
bloodshed
and atrocities.
Reach out,
and bring peace to our broken world.

We think of those who have fled as refugees,
living often in squalor with poor sanitation,
little food
and basic accommodation,
camps rife with disease and malnutrition.
And we think also of those who have left as migrants,
in search of a better life,
taking incalculable risks to do so,
yet fearful of what sort of reception they will receive
if and when they reach their destination.
Reach out,
and bring peace to our broken world.

We think of victims of war –
the dead,
the dying,
the injured,

the suffering –
and we pray for their families and loved ones:
those who grieve,
who fear for their welfare,
who seek to support and comfort.
Reach out,
and bring peace to our broken world.

We think of world leaders and governments,
politicians, diplomats and ambassadors –
all involved in putting pressure on warring forces to end
combat and make peace.
And we think of members of the armed forces when they
are deployed to this end,
risking life and limb in far-flung parts of the world,
far from home and family,
exposed to the trauma of battle.
Reach out,
and bring peace to our broken world.

We think of all who work for reconciliation and harmony –
between tribes,
races,
creeds,
cultures,
countries
and continents.
Help them truly to bring people together –
to change attitudes,
to challenge prejudice,
to overcome hatred,
and to build trust and unity.
Reach out,
and bring peace to our broken world.
Amen.

95. War, people and places broken by

(See also The armed forces; Peacemakers; War and peace; World peace)

God of all,
hear our prayer today for those whose lives have been shattered by war.

To those whose livelihoods have been destroyed,
bring hope.

To those who homes have been devastated,
bring hope.

To those driven as refugees from their country,
bring hope.

To those who have lost family, partners, parents, children, loved ones,
bring hope.

To those who have suffered injury, abuse, persecution or torture,
bring hope.

To those who live in fear for their lives,
bring hope.

To those whose towns and cities have been shattered beyond recognition,
bring hope.

To those who have known nothing else but hatred,
violence and bloodshed,
bring hope.

To those whom war has left starving,
bring hope.

To those facing disease and despair as a result of conflict,
bring hope.

To those who see no hope of a resolution to conflict,
no prospect of peace,
bring hope.
Amen.

96. World, seeking real and lasting change in

(*See also* Barriers in society, those working to break down; Peacemakers; Social justice; World peace)

God of all,
though it feels sometimes as though we pray for it in vain,
hear our prayer for real and lasting change in our world.

Hear our prayer for peace:
an end to conflict and violence,
and to everything that leads to division between person
and person,
culture and culture,
creed and creed,
nation and nation.
Though so little seems to change,
help us to keep believing it can happen.

Hear our prayer for justice:
an end to exploitation of so many in our world who daily
face starvation,
abject poverty,
avoidable sickness and disease,
unimaginable privations.
Though so little seems to change,
help us to keep believing it can happen.

Hear our prayer for dialogue:
an end to the prejudices that prevent people
from coming together in a spirit of love,
cooperation,
respect
and understanding;
to the evils of discrimination on the basis of race, sex,
gender or conviction.
Though so little seems to change,
help us to keep believing it can happen.

Hear our prayer for new beginnings:
an end to all that causes people to lose hope in themselves,
in society,
in life
or in you.
Though so little seems to change,
help us to keep believing it can happen.

Help us to keep believing that though change is slow,
and not always for the best,
we can still strive towards a better world,
a brighter future for all.
Though so little seems to change,
help us to keep believing it can happen.
Amen.

97. World leaders

(See also Governments and world leaders)

Lord of all,
hear our prayer for world leaders.

In a world of economic recession,
grant wisdom.

In a world of rich and poor,
grant wisdom.

In a world beset by war and hatred,
grant wisdom.

In a world scarred by extremism and hatred,
grant wisdom.

In a world of increasingly intolerant nationalism,
grant wisdom.

In a world where prejudice and discrimination
are all too real,
grant wisdom.

In a world of greed and corruption,
grant wisdom.

In a world where giant corporations wield excessive power,
grant wisdom.

In a world where illness and disease still blight
the lives of many,
grant wisdom.

In a world of global warming, climate change
and environmental destruction,
grant wisdom.

In a world of homelessness and refugees,
grant wisdom.

In a world where thousands still die of starvation,
grant wisdom.

In a world of natural and manmade disasters,
grant wisdom.

In a world of political intrigue and machinations,
grant wisdom.

To leaders everywhere, entrusted with such onerous
challenges and responsibilities,
grant wisdom.
Amen.

98. World peace

(See also Barriers in society, those working to break down;
The armed forces; The Middle East; Peacemakers; War and
peace; War, people and places broken by)

Lord of all,
we pray once more for peace in our world,
for harmony between nations,
for reconciliation where there is division,
for cooperation where there is confrontation,
for a willingness to resolve conflict through dialogue
rather than through force.
Whatever keeps people apart,
may more draw them together.

We pray for those who live in the shadow of war –
those who live each day in fear and uncertainty,
whose homes and livelihoods have been destroyed,
whose loved ones have been killed,
who have had to flee from their country as refugees.
Whatever keeps people apart,
may more draw them together.

We pray for those who attempt to initiate peace
in troubled parts of our world –
regions racked by discord and division,
hatred and suspicion,
political and religious divides.
Whatever keeps people apart,
may more draw them together.

We pray for politicians and negotiators,
leaders and rulers –
all with power to help effect change.
Give them wisdom,
compassion,
courage
and vision,
so that they may act fairly,
and promote lasting peace acceptable to all.
Whatever keeps people apart,
may more draw them together.
Amen.

99. The worried

(See also The anxious; Trouble, those facing times of (1) and (2))

God of all,
hear our prayer for the troubled and fearful –
those for whom thoughts of the present or the future fill
them with anxiety.

We think of those who question whether they will be able
to cope with what life brings them:
those worried about themselves or their loved ones;
those wrestling with irrational phobias;
those facing problems to which they can see no solution;
those imprisoned by secret fears that they struggle
to admit to themselves,
let alone to others.
Grant peace.
Grant confidence.

We think of those worried about money,
health,
work,
relationships –
those wrestling with debt or cash flow,
unsure how they will pay their way;
those who are unwell or who are awaiting a diagnosis;
those unable to cope with their jobs
or who fear they might lose them;
those experiencing marital breakdown,
estrangement from loved ones,
or simply the spectre of loneliness.
Grant peace.
Grant confidence.

We pray for those who seek to help those who are anxious:
to share their load in some way,
to offer them comfort and support,
to talk through problems
or simply to be a friend in time of need.
Grant peace.
Grant confidence.

To all whose lives are in turmoil,
racked by difficulties and worries that threaten
to overwhelm them,
give help,
give strength,
give reassurance –
tranquillity of spirit and calmness of mind.
Grant peace.
Grant confidence.
Amen.

100. Young people

(*See also* Children leaving home)

Lord of all,
hear our prayer for young people.

We think of children growing up,
facing the challenge of school and exams,
of learning more about themselves
and the world around them,
of gradually growing towards maturity.
To all young people,
give help on their journey.

We think of the opportunities yet pressures
young people face today:
the possibilities that our online world opens up,
giving access to all kinds of resources as never before,
but also the problems –
the danger of cyber-bullying and stalking,
of online gambling, pornography or scams,
of developing virtual relationships at the cost of real ones,
of being so wedded to their phone, tablet or computer
that they have little time for anything else.
To all young people,
give help on their journey.

We think of the challenges every young person must meet:
of leaving the security of home
and striking out on their own;
of finding employment and building a career;
of adjusting to university or college life
or to the demands of the workplace;

of finding a partner and establishing new relationships.
To all young people,
give help on their journey.

We think of young people for whom life is hard:
those who have learning difficulties;
those who are disabled
or who are fighting serious illness;
those from broken homes;
those in countries torn by war and hatred;
and those who have been orphaned.
To all young people,
give help on their journey.

We think of young people denied the innocence
of childhood or happiness of youth:
those who are sexually abused,
mistreated,
unloved,
deprived
or bullied.
And we think of those who minister in such situations –
doctors, social workers, psychiatrists and counsellors –
all who strive to heal the wounds and lessen the scars.
To all young people,
give help on their journey.
Amen.

Other books of intercessions by Nick Fawcett

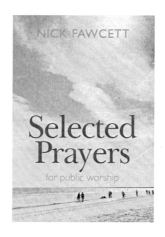

Selected Prayers for Public Worship
1500586

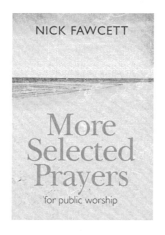

More Selected Prayers for Public Worship
1501398

You'll find a comprehensive collection of Nick's books at
www.kevinmayhew.com